Simon Says . . .
"Reading Is Fun!"

Movement-Based Activities to Reinforce Beginning Reading Skills

Tabatha A. Uhrich
Monica McHale-Small

A SCARECROWEDUCATION BOOK

The Scarecrow Press, Inc.
Lanham, Maryland, and London
2002

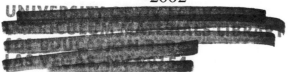

A SCARECROWEDUCATION BOOK

Published in the United States of America
by Scarecrow Press, Inc.
A Member of the Rowman & Littlefield Publishing Group
4720 Boston Way
Lanham, Maryland 20706
www.scarecroweducation.com

4 Pleydell Gardens, Folkestone
Kent CT20 2DN, England

British Library Cataloguing in Publication Information Available

Library of Congress Cataloging-in-Publication Data
Uhrich, Tabatha A., 1967–
    Simon says—"Reading is fun!" : movement-based activities to reinforce beginning
  reading skills / Tabatha A. Uhrich, Monica McHale-Small.
        p. cm.
    Includes bibliographical references and index.
    ISBN 0-8108-4208-4 (pbk. : alk. paper)
        1. Reading games. 2. Reading (Primary) I. McHale-Small, Monica, 1960– II. Title.

LB1525.55 .U57 2002
372.4—dc21

                                                                    2001057558

♾️™ The paper used in this publication meets the minimum requirements
of American National Standard for Information Sciences—Permanence of
Paper for Printed Library Materials, ANSI/NISO Z39.48-1992.
Manufactured in the United States of America.

For my mom, Reta J. Bingmer.
—*Tabatha A. Uhrich*

For my children, Alexandra, James, Kevin, and Owen.
—*Monica McHale-Small*

Contents

The inspiration for this book was the involvement of one of the authors in an intensive remedial program for first grade students struggling with beginning reading skills. "First Grade Groups," as it was known at our school, brought together a team of professionals from various disciplines to design and implement interventions that would develop early literacy skills. Tab Uhrich, the school's physical education teacher, was asked to use her skills to design games and activities that would teach the children directional and spatial concepts and body awareness, including the names of body parts.

Because the purpose of the intervention was to remediate early reading skills, it did not take long for the activities in the gym to develop into games that directly taught and reinforced letter and sound identification as well as sight words. When both the authors were involved in a summer reading program for children completing grades one through four, the number of games grew considerably. It was at this time that we began to talk about compiling the games and activities so that we could share them with our colleagues.

The following school year, a group of kindergarten students was selected to receive a little extra practice with letters and sounds. We found that some of the games we had used during the summer program as well as some that had been successful with the first graders were just a little too difficult or involved for the kindergarten students. A new group of activities and games was developed or adapted for use with these younger students. It was probably the reaction of these youngest students to the activities in the gym that convinced us that the games were definitely worth sharing.

The kindergarten students who needed the extra practice with letters also tended to be the more active students in the classroom. These children relished the extra opportunity to be in an environment where they could run and jump and be noisy. We loved watching just how engaged these students were in learning when given the opportunity to move. When our search for more activities and ideas for these obviously kinesthetic learners yielded little, we knew that what we had developed needed to be shared.

Simon Says . . . "Reading Is Fun!" is a compilation of all the games and activities we have used with children. Typically, we have worked with students in groups ranging in size from eight to fifteen. When working with students who are struggling, small groups and more than one adult will certainly maximize the benefit and increase the time that each student is engaged with tasks at his or her instructional level. While our purpose has been to intervene with students who are below grade level, it is important to note that many of these activities can be used successfully with whole class groups. The gym has been the primary setting for our use of these activities because it is a comfortable place within the school for movement and noise. We have, however, also used classrooms, hallways, and the outdoors with great success. It is our hope that those of you who choose to use the *Simon Says . . . "Reading Is Fun!"* activities will do so in a variety of settings, in creative ways and with many different students.

Acknowledgments

We would like to take the opportunity to acknowledge and thank those who have in some way contributed to this book. It was Todd Gardner's and Gwen Thelen's recognition of the importance of a movement component to the education of the whole child that led to the initial invitation to Tab Uhrich to be a part of Union Canal School's first grade remedial reading intervention. "First Grade Groups" was the original context for the development of the games and activities in this book. Thanks to Todd and Gwen for their origination and organization of this intervention program and to Elaine Stine as well, for her later contributions.

We would like to express our sincere gratitude to our former principal, Rebecca Hostetler, for her enthusiastic support of *Simon Says . . . "Reading Is Fun!"* throughout its development and in all of its venues. Becky has been a mentor and friend to us both. Thanks to Suanna Sparkman for serving as a sounding board for our ideas and encouraging us to move forward. Alice Oskam has provided us with her reading expertise and has been our number one cheerleader. Thanks to all of the primary teachers and students at Union Canal; without their support and participation, this project would not have been possible.

Finally, we would like to thank all of our family and friends who encouraged, supported, and assisted us as *Simon Says . . . "Reading Is Fun!"* developed from an idea to a book of activities.

CHAPTER 1

Introduction and Rationale

Visit almost any public school in the United States right now, and you will no doubt hear about the push for early literacy. The fact that kindergarten is no longer "fun and games" has been a slowly evolving reality. Academically oriented kindergartens were surely legitimized by the Reading Excellence Act, which proclaims that all children must come to school "ready to learn" and that teachers must "provide children with the readiness skills they need to learn once they enter school."[1] In their quest to have all children reading well before they enter fourth grade, more and more schools are demanding that children as young as five sit quietly as they are "taught" the skills they will need to start reading, a goal that they hope will be achieved before the end of kindergarten. Those children who cannot or will not comply with the demands of their teachers are deemed "not ready to learn" and are recommended for "solutions" ranging from grade retention to special education. Rarely do we educators stop and think that it may well be that the schools are not ready for the students.[2]

The University of Idaho's Center on Developmental Disabilities stresses that the theory of emergent literacy should replace the traditional concept of reading and writing readiness. This theory recognizes that early literacy encompasses much more than learning letters, sounds, and sight words. The foundation of literacy is the child's ability to understand and later use language. It involves the child's very early "reading" skills such as the infant's or toddler's ability to recognize signs, labels, and logos. Children develop literacy through a series of specific stages, which should not be skipped or glossed over.[3] Early literacy develops in a language- and symbol-rich environment. Sometimes this environment is missing or limited at home due to a variety of factors, including poverty and parents' own low literacy levels. Children who have not had the advantage of a language-rich environment prior to coming to school should not be penalized or treated as failures. It is up to the school to meet the needs of the child who is at an emergent literacy level.

In a perfect world, that is exactly what would happen. Schools would meet children where they are and guide them to new places. Unfortunately, we do not live in a perfect world. Many schools insist on trying to make the child fit the program rather than vice versa. When he or she doesn't, the blame is placed within the child or with the, home environment. Children who fail to learn in the way we want them to are referred to special education or remedial programs. If the reality is going to be that we insist that all children learn the same thing at the same time, then we should at least increase the chances for success by teaching skills in ways that fit the learners.

The games and activities in this book are designed mindful of the needs of those beginning readers who aren't quite ready to sit quietly and learn the skills the schools say they must. This book is full of activities that teach and reinforce letters, sounds, sight words, phonemic skills, and spatial concepts while allowing for plenty of movement. To the untrained eye, these activities may well look like "fun and games." Since fun and games have been all but banned in some schools as they pursue academic excellence, we will briefly summarize some of the research and theories that lend support to the use of these activities. Hopefully, what follows will be enough to convince the skeptic.

LEARNING STYLES AND MULTIPLE INTELLIGENCES

The literature devoted to learning styles and multiple intelligences offers plenty of support for the games and activities described in this book. Gardner wrote in *The Disciplined Mind*, "I believe in action and activity. The brain learns best and retains most when the organism is actively involved in exploring physical sites and materials."[4]

Research suggests that at least 25 percent of the general population is composed of kinesthetic/tactile learners. Armstrong notes that bodily kinesthetic learners think in terms of somatic sensations. They love dancing, running, jumping, and touching. To learn best, these students need movement, physical games, and tactile, hands-on learning experiences.[5] In other words, these children need the activities on the pages to follow.

The early childhood education literature is chock-full of activities that will entice visual, auditory, spatial, and linguistic learners. Hundreds of art projects, chants, songs, and picture books are available for teaching letters, sounds, and sight words. Dozens of ideas provide plenty of input for tactile learners; for example, sand writing, shaving cream, and even pudding have been favorites for years. We have found that there is surprisingly little available, however, for those learners who need bodily/kinesthetic input to optimize their learning.

Those who have spent significant time around preschool and early elementary children will readily attest to the fact that children this age do not enjoy sitting for very long. In fact, movement is one of the things that characterizes young children. Certainly there are individual differences in learning styles, but there are, no doubt, developmental differences as well. Young children are by their very nature kinesthetic. Werner theorizes that human development entailed moving from a very global state of being to one in which cognitive processes are differentiated and distinct. For young children, thought, perception, motor action, and emotion are relatively undifferentiated.[6] Young children "do" life with their whole body. They run through it, jump in it, roll across it, and crawl over it. So often in schools we try to force children to sit still and listen attentively when they are simply unable to do so for any extended period of time. If we must teach letters and sounds and words to four, five, and six year olds, then let's do it in a way that allows them to experience these concepts with their whole bodies.

Snow reminds us that these wigglers and shakers enjoy movement and are widely misunderstood in the highly structured world of education.[7] Perhaps, then, it is no coincidence that research is increasingly indicating that such learners make up the majority of those students labeled "at risk."[8] When Stone used *The Learning Styles Inventory*[9] to learn more about the students in his low-achieving elementary school, he found that 64 percent of the students were kinesthetic or tactile learners, while only 21 percent were auditory; the type of learner best suited for traditional teaching methods. A sizable 34 percent of the student body felt they needed to move around frequently. When Stone and his staff altered instructional methods, lighting, and even timing of instruction to match the needs of the students, they reported dramatic improvement in academic achievement.[10]

Often, attempts to meet the needs of kinesthetic learners in public schools, if they happen at all, simply involve more opportunities to get up and take a walk around the classroom or school. Some studies report things like "mobility footprints" on the floor or an exercise bike to be used during movement breaks.[11] The advantage of the activities in this book is that they allow for movement and academic practice simultaneously.

The children with whom these games and activities have been developed tended to be the "movers and shakers" in their classrooms. While the most fidgety of students probably have had the most to gain from the use of our games and activities, all types of students can enjoy and benefit from them. Educators have known for centuries that we remember best not what we see or hear but what we do. Remember, "I hear and I forget; I see and I remember; I do and I understand."[12]

BRAIN RESEARCH

Brain research and *brain-based learning* are terms that are popping up in educational literature with increasing frequency. We hesitate to point to brain research as a justification for our activities. To many, the combination of movement activities and reading instruction causes flashbacks to the days when children who were struggling to learn to read were sent to the gym to walk on balance beams. It could conjure up thoughts of Delacato's psychomotor patterning, a popular "treatment" for learning disabilities and mental retardation.[13] Or, maybe skepticism has been created by somewhat more recent claims that a series of movements such as neck rolls, belly breathing, and foot flexing will translate into quicker acquisition of reading skills.[14]

Fortunately, the claims of recent "brain theory educators" are more modest and plausible. The focus is on using what science has taught us about the relationship between the brain and the environment, and the news is good for more active and playful approaches to teaching. Jensen makes a case for incorporating more opportunities for movement and requiring less sitting of students from kindergarten through graduate school. He sights evidence from psychology, neurology, ergonomics, and kinesiology to support the benefits of physical activity to the learning process. Jensen notes that the increased arousal that results from movement helps to focus our attention to specific tasks.[15] He cites research suggesting that movement around a room allows for more learning locations, which results in episodic encoding and enhanced spatial learning.[16] Jensen asserts that active, movement-based learning opportunities result in learning that is "longer lasting, better remembered, more fun, age appropriate, intelligence independent and that reaches more kinds of learners."[17]

Caine and Caine do not directly argue for more movement in the classroom, but some of the assertions they do make could be considered arguments for the use of the games and activities outlined in this book. The Caines cite the role of emotions in the learning process.[18] The idea that fear, tension, and fatigue inhibit learning while a relaxed state coupled with appropriate challenge enhance it may be all the justification one needs to make use of the ideas in this book. Few who have spent any significant time around young children could assert that there is a more relaxed state for a child than the state of play.

To learn a new skill we must be attentive, reasonably relaxed, and engaged in the task at hand.[19] When students are using all of their energy to stifle movement and remain seated, when they are working hard to remained focused on something they find to be intrinsically boring and tedious, they naturally have less energy available to them to devote to the learning of a new skill. If we can lessen the energy demands by using instructional strategies that allow for movement and that pique the interest and excitement of the child, we assure that more brain power is being devoted to the skill to be learned.

PLAY AND DEVELOPMENT

The games and activities in this book are purposeful but playful as well. Play has been central to early childhood education since Friedrich

Froebel established the first kindergarten in 1837. In 1929, Issacs proclaimed play to be the child's work.[20] With plenty of backing from developmental theorists both before and since, Issacs and other educators helped to cement play into the foundation of early childhood educational practice. Vygotsky saw the social context of play as a medium for learning and internalizing cultural values and mores. He, like Piaget after him, recognized children's play as an arena for the construction of knowledge and for the development and practice of new skills.[21]

As we have moved into the information processing age, and calls for educational reform of all sorts have echoed louder, the cement has begun to crumble and play's place in the classroom has become less secure. In fact, the push for early literacy seems to have resulted in a jackhammer being taken to the last remaining bits of play to make room for more direct instruction of skills. Many school districts seem to hold a belief that unless an activity involves paper, pencils, or print, it is not related to literacy. In an attempt to assure "all students are reading by the third grade,"[22] activities such as free play, snack time, and craft projects have been curtailed in favor of explicit instruction in letters, sounds, print concepts, and phonological and phonemic processes.

What seems to have been forgotten is just what Vygotsky, Piaget, and others told us so long ago. That is, the social context of play and opportunities for children to manipulate objects in their world in playful and creative ways allows for the development of the language skills and cognitive concepts that are crucial for later literacy. Allowing play into the classroom does not mean that academic goals must be sacrificed. A housekeeping corner, a longtime kindergarten favorite, can be stocked with telephone memo pads, blank recipe cards, cookbooks, and shopping lists and thus afford numerous opportunities for children to interact with print. By joining in the play, the teacher can model the function and importance of print.[23] Countless games also can be used to teach counting and numerical concepts. Playfulness is what makes learning fun.

The type of play constructivist educators advocate for is child directed and open-ended. With the pressure to have all children reading early in their academic careers, it may well be that this type of play has seen its day in public schools. Nonetheless, what young children like to do best is to play. So, why not use what children like as a tool for teaching them? The games and activities in this book are teacher directed and designed to teach or to practice specific skills and concepts. To the children involved in them, they are indeed "play and games," and that is all that is important.

We started this chapter by arguing that the activities within are more than fun and games. It may just be, however, that the biggest advantage of these activities is that they are indeed play and games. Play may or may not be the work of the child, but one thing is for sure: turning "work" into "play" is a guaranteed way to accomplish more work.

NOTES

1. Reading Excellence Act 1999, http://www.ed.gov/offices/OSE/REA/overview.html, accessed 10 February 2001.

2. Susan Black, "The First Two R's," *American School Board Journal* 186, no. 10 (1999): 44–46.

3. Black, "The First Two R's," 45.

4. Howard Gardner, *The Disciplined Mind* (New York: Basic Books, 1999), 82.

5. Thomas Armstrong, *Multiple Intelligences in the Classroom* (Alexandria, Va.: Association for Supervision and Curriculum Development, 1994).

6. John H. Flavell, *Cognitive Development*, 2d ed. (Englewood Cliffs, N.J.: Prentice Hall, 1985), 31–33.

7. Rebecca Snow, "Learning Styles in Young Children," 1999, http://earlychildhood.miningco.com/, accessed 10 February 2001.

8. Rita Dunn and Kenneth Dunn, *Teaching Elementary Students through Their Individual Learning Styles: Practical Approaches for Grades 3–6* (Boston: Allyn & Bacon, 1993).

9. Rita Dunn, Kenneth Dunn, and G. E. Price, *Learning Styles Inventory* (Lawrence, Kans.: Price Systems, 1990).

10. Pete Stone, "How We Turned Around a Problem School," *Principal* 72, no. 2 (1992): 34–36.

11. A. Braio et al., "Incremental Implementation of Learning Style Strategies among Urban Low Achievers," *Journal of Educational Research* 91, no. 3 (1997): 15–25.

12. Old Chinese proverb, source unknown.

13. Charles Delacato, *The Diagnosis and Treatment of Speech and Reading Problems* (Springfield, Ill.: Thomas, 1963).

14. Paul Dennison and Gail Dennison, *Brain Gym: Teacher's Edition, Revised* (Ventura, Calif.: Edu-Kinesthetics, 1989).

15. Eric Jensen, "Moving with the Brain," *Educational Leadership* 58, no. 3 (2000): 37.

16. Jensen, "Moving with the Brain," 35.

17. Jensen, "Moving with the Brain," 37.

18. Renate Nummela Caine and Geoffrey Caine, "Brain Based Learning: How the Brain Works," 1994, http://www.cainelearning.com, accessed 10 February 2001.

19. Caine and Caine, "Brain Based Learning."

20. S. Issacs, *The Nursery Years* (London: Routledge & Kegan Paul, 1929), quoted in Anthony Pelligrini, ed., *The Future of Play Theory* (Albany: State University of New York Press, 1995), 11.

21. Flavell, *Cognitive Development,* 58.

22. Reading Excellence Act 1999.

23. Judith Kieff and Renée Casbergue, *Playful Learning and Teaching: Integrating Play into Preschool and Primary Programs* (Boston: Allyn & Bacon, 2000).

CHAPTER 2

For Teachers

FOR PHYSICAL EDUCATION TEACHERS

The activities in this book are a means to support the reading instruction provided in the classroom; they are not a method to teach how to read. Naturally, the better one knows and understands the process of reading, the greater the chance of impact in the use of these activities with your students. The games and activities may be a supplement to other games and activities used in the classroom for kinesthetic learners or possibly the only opportunity for kinesthetic learning to take place for the beginning reader. It is wise to stay in touch with the reading instructors in your school setting, to be sure that you are reinforcing the same concepts as they are reinforcing in their classrooms. Furthermore, they will be able to guide you in the progress of the students with whom you are working and help to individualize instruction.

Individualized Instruction

Individualized instruction is an important component in all areas of instruction. Although many students can be taught by the same means of instruction, not all students are at the same starting point with their knowledge. Understanding this concept and taking the time to bring students to the starting blocks with your instructional treatment is one of the hallmarks of a good teacher. Knowing that the concept of individualized instruction is an ongoing process is equally important; we do not, as teachers, attempt to bring all students to the same place before beginning instruction and then expect that all of our students will follow us neatly along our teaching path. Students are going to miss some of the things we say, do, and teach; students are going to be absent; students are going to catch some of this and some of that and require your help to piece it all together. Individualizing instruction is like a thread that runs all through the teaching process: it should always be present. Our job is continually to monitor—through casual observation, informal and formal assessment— the progress of our students and, when necessary, apply individual instruction to bring the students along, as they are developmentally able to do so.

The activities in this book, along with the ones you adapt and create to accompany your early literacy instruction, are meant to be used as tools; again, they are not instruction itself but tools to accompany the instruction. Each activity may be used differently and at different times, depending on your students' needs. At times, all students might be engaged in the same activity, with the same learning objective. Many times, all students will be engaged in the same activity, with different learning objectives for different students. Sometimes, the learning activities will vary as well as the learning objectives, within the same instructional period.

Individualizing instruction is sometimes as easy as redirecting or reminding a student of the letter, sound, or sight word they learned earlier. Other times it is a mystery in which you are the detective, gathering information on the student's early literacy history, learning style, classroom assessment, and your own observations and assessments. The work of the detective is what we do in our class all the time, usually in the psychomotor domain. In this vein, you are simply transferring your detective skills to a new domain. In the process, you are not only helping your students to become better readers, or more skilled in the process of learning to read, but you are also learning more about the teaching of these early literacy skills. In searching out the solution to a student's dilemma, you might increase your knowledge base about literacy, increase the amount of ways to teach an early literacy skill, or learn more about a particular student's learning style. All of this information will transfer to helping not only the struggling student but also all students thereafter who experience difficulty in a similar manner.

Basic Understandings

Some basic understandings will help you to be more effective at the outset in using these activities. Students will be able to recognize letters before identifying them by name. Students will be able to recognize letters before they will be able to tell the sound of given letters. Of course, these are generalizations, as some students may surprise you by being able to recognize a letter and give its sound. Students will be able to match like letters before being able to identify a given letter from a pile of letters. Students might be more successful at identifying a given letter from a pile of letters than by telling the sound of the given letter. Knowing this information will help you to find a starting point in activity selection. A kindergartner in the fall of the year would be more likely to benefit from a letter-matching game than an activity in which the students are to find the letter that matches the sound given. First grade students in the spring of the year may be perfectly happy spelling sight words, using an Alphabet Sea to allow them to run for the letters, rather than playing a matching game. In your detective work, you will find out what students need, then provide that game or activity. See chapter 4 for a further breakdown of early literacy skills.

Alternative Content

You may find that students need a break from the early literacy activities. They may still be willing to run, play, shout, and learn, but the content or information needs to be changed. Using your own creativity, alter the activities and games as you see fit. Always remember, "It is about the students."[1] Our job is to teach the students, and sometimes we need to learn from them first to do our job. Learning from them may mean altering a game or activity to increase or decrease the competitive level to keep them engaged. Learning from the students may mean changing one or more aspects of the activity, to alleviate boredom. What seems fun to us may not always seem fun to them. Be observant, as you would in your psychomotor domain, to the needs of the students. Activities that reinforce colors, directionality terms, body parts, and students' addresses, phone numbers, and middle names are common themes we have used in the past to increase the students' knowledge base while differentiating content.

We have found that many of the students who benefit from additional help with early literacy skills combined with kinesthetic movement are often the students who do not know their middle names, phone numbers, or addresses. It is obviously important for students to know these items. Once the students have learned this information, it can be used for practicing letter identification, letter recognition, and sound identification.

We have played a game in which the students may enter the gym if they can answer the question correctly. The question might be "What is your middle name?" "What is your full name?" "What is your phone number?" "What is your address?" "What day of the week is it?" "What month is it?" "What is today's date?" "What is the season?" "What year is it?" It may seem like basic information that we take for granted, but the children who hear the season, date, day of week, and weather in their classroom meeting at the start of the day may easily forget by the next hour. Of course, all students are admitted to the gym, whether they readily know the answer or need help, but this little game gives one more opportunity for review. These pieces of information are what we use to track awareness. Awareness is essential to attending, and unless you are attending, there is no learning. If the students haven't picked up this information somewhere along the way, there may be a reason for it.

You may make the difference with the kinesthetic approach. Sitting in a circle while the teacher or fellow students discuss the weather and date may seem very boring to an itchy, active child who is spending all of his or her energy trying to sit still. Others may be disinterested in the conversation and look longingly out the window wishing for recess or daydreaming. These students need to be as aware as the others in the classroom as to the date, weather, season, address, phone number, and full name. Reaching them with this information, however, may need to occur in a different type of setting or by different means than that classroom meeting. Again, this is where these kinesthetic games and activities may make the difference. Finally, directionality terms and body parts are equally important to the physical education curriculum and parallel the delivery of this content in both curricula.

Affect

Your curriculum is the link between you and the students with whom you will be working with these early literacy games and activities. The students have already met you and experienced you as a physical education teacher, and they are acquainted with the gymnasium, equipment, and movement. Your rapport with them will carry you far in helping reach the literacy-related objectives. Most children enjoy physical education and look forward to being in an atmosphere where they can do what kids like to do—play, run, move. Hopefully, students will be eager to engage in your environment with these activities, too. Your approach is important, as it is with the psychomotor domain.

Your philosophy is probably one that includes the affective component, in which you not only strive to teach safety and sportsmanship but also maintain an environment where all students like to participate and look forward to your class. The same qualities that bring about this enthusiasm are the same ones you want to instill with these early literacy games and activities. The ultimate goal is to get students to read; whatever we must do as educators to meet that goal is our mission.

Where the onus was once on the first grade teacher alone, we now share the duty. As recent as the late 1990s, the typical kindergarten class consisted of play, school preparedness, and learning letters and sounds. The kindergarten we once knew has quickly been replaced with academic skills that may frown on play. The role of the kindergarten teacher has changed, and he or she now shares a greater duty in teaching literacy, as do many of the other educators in the elementary setting. The physical education teacher has a pivotal role to play for the kinesthetic learners, if not all students.

A key to success in the use of these games and activities is patience. Remember that some of the activities and games you select to play with the students may not be the correct ones you need for the level of your students. You won't know until you set up the activity, show the students how to play, and then observe. Be overly prepared, at least in the beginning, so that if an activity is too easy or too difficult for some or all of the students, you have alternate plans. This approach will save you from discipline problems, resulting from work that is too easy or too frustrating for your students. For some of you, the students you will work with will be students who have already experienced frustration in the classroom with early literacy content. Although the content and delivery are new to you, they may already be a source of pain and discomfort for struggling students. In addition, your "hit or miss" lesson plans while attempting to assess the level of the students may make for some frustrating instructional periods. Remember that you are not offering the reading instruction, which is happening in the classroom; rather, you are providing support for the students who have had difficulty.

Another key to success is sensitivity and open-mindedness. A student who identifies a letter incorrectly may have simply inverted it. The student who is shown the lowercase *"d"* but identifies it as a *"b"* probably has already heard "No, that is wrong." Offering words of encouragement with corrective feedback such as "You are close—try turning the letter the other way" will go a lot further in helping the child to learn the name of the letter than letting her flounder in her error with no way of knowing how to correct herself. If you teach the students to turn the letter around and look at it differently, they may come to understand more quickly how to solve errors, when they make them, than when given negative feedback but no instruction for correction. Remember, it is about the students, and the goal is to get them to read.

A similar example occurred in an activity in which students were given a Word Card and sent out to the Alphabet Sea to retrieve the needed letters to form the given word on the card. A little boy had the word *"dog"* written on his card, in lowercase handwriting. He retrieved the correct letters and promptly laid them out to form the word *"god."* A fifth grade student who was assisting went over to help him to see his error, when Tab noticed that the boy had indeed found his letters and spelled his word correctly. You see, I was watching from across the floor, where I saw that my letters looked like *"god"* instead of *"dog"* when looked at upside down. The way I had handed the Word Card to the little boy showed *"god,"* so he was correct all along. We must be open-minded to our students as they learn. I, too, learned that day, that I must be open-minded, as well as more clear when creating Word Cards and other tools used in my classroom.

FOR CLASSROOM TEACHERS

Neither of us are classroom teachers, but we have both spent enough time in schools and in classrooms to know that many of these games and activities are workable in a classroom setting. In fact, a number of the activities were successfully undertaken with an entire class group within the confines of a classroom space. Some of the activities work best in a large space like the school's gym where there is plenty of room to move and be noisy. But, if you can be comfortable with a little more noise and more action, desks can be pushed aside, and lots of fun can be had while learning. If you aren't comfortable rearranging the furniture in your classroom, remember there is always the hallway or outdoors (weather permitting). The school gym, cafeteria, or even the stage may be empty and available at some point in the day.

Many of the games and activities can be kept short and incorporated into your language arts time for review and practice of skills already taught. If you are a kindergarten or first grade teacher using stations, some of the *Simon Says . . . "Reading Is Fun!"* activities can be readily adapted to fit your station time and space. In fact, in the gym we have had several activities going at once in stations set up around the room. Memory can easily fit into a corner of your classroom, as can Jump Rope Round-up. Mystery Writer is a fun and novel way for first and second grade students to practice spelling words and it requires little to no extra space.

Extra pairs of eyes and hands always make the activities run more smoothly but are at a premium is school settings. One thing you may want to think about is devising a way to allow older students to help younger ones. In our school, fifth grade and kindergarten lunch times overlapped. We were lucky to have a number of fifth grade students who volunteered some of their free time at lunch to be fifth grade tutors. These tutors came to the gym twice each week with their assigned kindergarten student in tow. They spent about fifteen minutes working with their students. We selected the activities and had the materials ready to go. Because we were keeping track of what letters, sounds, and words the students had mastered, we were able to compile sets of Alphabet and Word Cards with the right mix of new and already mastered letters or words for each individual student.

Many schools use older students as book buddies. This is where an intermediate-level class works with a primary class for the purpose of pairing older and younger students to read to one another. A whole school year's worth of weekly meetings has the potential of becoming a little mundane. *Simon Says . . . "Reading Is Fun!"* activities can be used to liven things up. Again, having an older student paired up with a younger one will make your job easier. You always want to make sure to have the materials selected and gathered. You will also need to carefully explain the activity or game and their role as "helper" or "tutor" to the older students.

As a classroom teacher, you are already well aware of how crucial to your students' success it is to individualize instruction to their specific needs and strengths. The *Simon Says . . . "Reading Is Fun!"* activities are ideal in that they are so adaptable. The same activity, using the same materials, can be used with the child who is just learning to match two like letters and at the same time with the child who is using letters to create words. Because everyone is using the same materials in a similar way, nobody is asking why he or she can't do what the others are doing. And, because everyone is working at his or her own level, each student is actively and happily engaged in the learning task. Preceding the description of each game is a listing of the specific skills that can be addressed with that game or activity. We would like to draw your attention to chapter 4, where you can find a brief discussion of these skills and definitions of some of the terms we will be using.

We have found that because the opportunity to move addresses the needs of kinesthetic learners, certain students are more on task and participatory than they typically are in the traditional classroom setting. Often, these students experience a level of comfort that they don't always have in a setting where they must sit for prolonged periods and listen carefully. Feeling comfortable, they sometimes demonstrate skills and engage in learning in a way not always evidenced in the classroom setting. On more than one occasion, we have seen children who "don't know any letters" running and shouting through the entire alphabet. As classroom teachers, you are constantly adapting instruction to the individual needs of your students. Sometimes, to obtain the best picture of what our students know, we need to adapt assessment methods as well.

NOTE

1. From a lecture by Dr. Rick Swalm on 23 May 2001, in the class "The Analytic Study of Teaching," at Temple University, Philadelphia, Pa.

CHAPTER 3

For Parents

As a school psychologist and mother of four, one of us authors—Monica—has had the opportunity to sit at both sides of the parent–teacher conference table. I cannot even begin to count the number of times I have heard teachers imploring parents to spend more time working with their children at home on drill-and-practice activities such as flash cards. I do not care to count the number of arguments I have had with my own children as I have tried to engage them in such activities.

If I am to believe all of the conversations I have had with teachers, then I must conclude that the majority of teachers who are parents have been blessed with children who find joy in whipping through a pack of flash cards. Since I chose the field of psychology, I apparently don't get to have that kind of child. Not one of my four children was the type to learn things like letters or sight words or math facts quickly, and none of them particularly cared for flash cards. Instead, my children's forte is getting off track. Tangential conversations; questions about why I choose to write the letters in blue rather than red; bathroom breaks; water breaks; snack breaks; anything but those flash cards or spelling words! I have a child who can lose a pencil without ever leaving his seat at the kitchen table; the pencils just disappear into thin air.

As a parent, I know that there are children out there who can easily turn the teacher's promise of "ten minutes" of homework into a four-hour ordeal. Working with your children at home isn't always as easy as the teacher might have you believe. I remember when my daughter was in first grade and she was struggling to learn a list of sight words. She was frustrated and inattentive. I was frustrated and beginning to lose my patience. The word cards were tossed on the floor in frustration, and I suddenly remembered a suggestion I had heard at a workshop on adapting curriculum for struggling students.

The presenter had suggested throwing the flash cards (of any sort) up in the air. She shared that having the children run about the room, picking up the card and reading the word or solving the problem made the task less mundane and more gamelike. I hadn't remembered this until that moment of watching the entire stack of cards land and spread out across the kitchen floor. We got through the whole pack of cards in a matter of minutes when my fidgety little daughter was moving around while reviewing her words. The novelty of this particular activity eventually wore off, leaving me searching for new ways to motivate all of my children as they struggled with skills they found difficult.

My experience as a parent has taught me two important things: (1) by making learning fun, one accomplishes a whole lot more learning, and (2) always remember, in my role as school psychologist, to be sensitive to the fact that parents have their work cut out for them. Whether you are simply assisting in reviewing weekly spelling words or undertaking home schooling, this chapter will hopefully provide some helpful hints and suggestions for those of you who are taking up the challenge of working with your children at home.

LETTER IDENTIFICATION SKILLS

When trying to get children to learn letters, we—parents and teachers both—sometimes forget that there is a hierarchy of skills that must be considered. If we jump right in at the top of the hierarchy, we may well be dooming the child to failure and frustration. When teaching letters, we must first ensure that the child is able to perceive the difference between two letters. We have been looking at letters for so long that *p* and *b* and *n* and *h* are easily discriminated. But to a young child just beginning to learn letters, they can look frustratingly similar. So, begin teaching letters by having your child match them. Ideally, an initial matching activity would involve you holding up a letter, stating the name of the letter, and directing the child to find the letter. You can make this activity easier or harder by manipulating the number of letter cards and the degree of similarity between the letters (e.g., *p, a, c,* and *k* to make it easy, and *p, b, d,* and *q* to make it difficult). Research suggests that uppercase letters are more easily discriminated, especially by younger children.[1] It makes good sense, then, to begin with uppercase letters and move on to lowercase once those have been mastered.

You can have your child practice matching independently by scattering sets of Alphabet Letter Cards around the room and having her sort them into piles of like letters. However, when done this way, this is an exercise in matching symbols only. While this is an essential skill for letter identification, it is only a small part. The association of the symbol with the name and sound of the letter is what we are striving for, and your input is what strengthens that association. Here is how the dialogue between you and your child might go:

> Parent: This is an *A*. What is this?
> Child: *A*.
> Parent: Good, it's the letter *A*. Now, can you go find me an *A*?
> *Child finds the letter A.*
> Parent: Great, you found it! What letter is this?
> *Child gives a puzzled look*
> Parent: This is the letter *A*. What letter is this?
> Child: *A*.

If your child has more familiarity with the letter names such that she can sing the alphabet song or maybe can even name some letters, you might want to consider introducing the sound along with the letter. That dialogue might go something like this:

> Parent: This is an *A*. What is this?
> Child: *A*.
> Parent: *A* says /a/ like in apple. What does *A* say?
> Child: /a/.
> Parent: Good, *A* says /a/. Now, can you go find me an A?
> *Child finds the letter A.*
> Parent: Great, you found it! What letter is this?
> Child: *A*.
> Parent: Yes, this is the letter *A*—you found it. What sound does it make?
> *Child gives a puzzled look.*
> Parent: It says /a/, like in apple. What sound does *A* make?
> Child: /a/.

Reading is all about sound-symbol connections, so it makes sense to show your child this connection right from the beginning. When you tell your child the name of a letter, tell him the sound and a word that starts with that sound as well. But remember, the focus at this stage is on learning the letter names. If children can produce the sound, great! If not, just remind them of the sound. Adams cautions that for children with little exposure to print or those who are struggling with letter names, introducing the sound with the letter name may be confusing and counterproductive.[2] Use your best judgment; you know your child better than anyone.

Once your child has mastered the first level of the letter-learning hierarchy, matching, you can move onto finding. By this time, your child has probably had lots of exposure to the letter names and sounds, so you may well be able to say, "Find me an *A* or find me the letter that says /a/." When your child is successful say, "Yes, that's right; it's an *A*. What is the name of this letter? What sound does it make?" Having your child repeat the name of the letter and make its sounds give her practice that will allow her to move more quickly to the final level of the hierarchy, letter naming.

We need to remember that it is, however, quite a big cognitive leap to go from recognizing a letter whose name children have been given to being able to recall and produce a letter name on demand. I can recount numerous incidents when I have been told by a teacher that a particular child doesn't know any letters. Yet when I present the child with a page of letters, I often find that this same child can point to most any letter I name.

Naming letters is the most difficult skill in the letter identification hierarchy. Some children are able to provide the sounds of letters before they can quickly and efficiently visually recognize and name the letters. It makes sense that a child who is having difficulty with the connecting and encoding of letter shapes with their names might have less trouble with sounds. Not only do the names of the letters often provide clues as to their sound, but they are also more meaningful. After all, words, which have meaning, are made up of letter sounds, not letter names. Most of us are better able to remember that which is meaningful. When teaching children, we often forget just how cognitively demanding the letter-naming task is. If we move too quickly to this very difficult skill without providing enough practice at the preceding levels, we are setting many children up for frustration and possible failure. Fluent and efficient letter-naming ability in kindergarten is an important predictor of later reading proficiency.[3] The more opportunities for practice of the skills leading up to the complex letter-naming task, the more likely children are to encode letter shapes and names firmly into their memories. The more firmly encoded, the more easily retrieved and the more fluent children will be at letter naming.

START SMALL AND BUILD ON SUCCESS

It is probably not an uncommon phenomenon for parents to one day be seized with panic when they realize that their child, who has never expressed any interest in learning letters, is just months away from starting kindergarten. I know firsthand that this panic can result in your announcing to your almost five year old that "Today is the day we learn the alphabet." This is, of course, an admirable but unrealistic goal. If your child has not initiated letter learning on his or her own and has not been expressing a whole lot of interest in letters and words, chances are your youngster is not going to pick up the whole alphabet in one day.

Beginning with the letters in your child's name is probably the best place to start. All of us are more motivated to learn things that are meaningful and relevant to our lives, and what word could possibly be more meaningful to your child than her name? Once your child masters the letters in his name, upper- and lowercase, add new letters, one or two at a time until you are eventually working with the whole alphabet. Cheney and Cohen suggest starting with the letters *Mm, Ff, Ss, Ww, Ll, Rr, Tt, Bb, Aa, Cc, Hh, Ii,* and *Pp,* because of their frequency of appearance in words and because they can be produced in isolation with the least amount of distortion.[4]

This is only one recommendation, and it may or may not be best for your child. If there is one particular letter that he always seems to get stuck on, I would consider putting that one away for a while. If the problem letter is one that happens to be in his name, then use an extra cue to help him. For example, when learning the letters in his name, my youngest son would always forget the letter *E*. When we came to that letter and he hesitated for more than a moment, I would cue him with

"It's that one you always forget." As we moved on to new letters that gave him trouble, new cues emerged: "It's that other tricky one" or "That's Kevin's letter." When we move on to sight words, cues might be necessary again. Each new set of words might have that one "really hard one."

Sometimes I would use a little play on words. When my children were stuck on the word *you,* I would say to them with exaggerated expression, "It's not me, it's . . . ." If I was still met with a blank stare, I would add some body language in the form of my finger pointing with dramatic flare directly at them as I ended my verbalization.

There is nothing wrong with providing extra cues for your child. Sometimes cues are looked at as a type of cheating, but our memories work by connecting new experiences and concepts with older, more familiar ones. Yes, we eventually want to get to a point where your child can name letters, produce sounds, and read sight words automatically. We need to remember that that is an end point we are working toward. In the meantime, we want your child to feel successful, and we want even more for her to be practicing correctly.

There is probably nothing worse or more confusing than practicing an error. Think of the child who must write his spelling words ten times each for homework. Now think of that same child writing one or more of his words incorrectly ten times. What has happened? The child has learned to spell the word incorrectly. The same type of thing can happen when a child identifies a letter or word incorrectly: an error is being practiced and learned. Or, think of the child who has no idea of a particular letter's name and randomly shouts a whole string of letters. In this case, no connection is being made that will help to cement the letter name into the child's memory. If your child hesitates for more than a second or two, give a cue or give the letter name or the word. As in the earlier dialogue, don't let your child flounder. If "What letter is this?" gets no response or an incorrect response, tell her, "This is an *A*. What letter is it?" When your child responds correctly, reinforce her immediately; "Yes, that's right—it's an *A*"; then ask again, "What letter is it?" The key is going to be lots of practice with lots of success. We need to ensure that your child is always practicing correctly even if that requires us giving him the letter name and having him repeat it over and over again. It may get tedious and frustrating for you as the parent, but one day your child will name it correctly and without hesitation. Be sure to celebrate this victory with hugs and praises!

Simon Says . . . "Reading Is Fun!" is filled with plenty of games and activities that will keep the practice fun and playful for your child and hopefully for you as well. Consider everything your child does with the letter *A:* finding an Alphabet Letter Card, making it with a jump rope, drawing it with chalk, positioning her body on the floor in the shape of an *A.* Each is yet another opportunity for that letter name or sound to imprint itself on your child's memory.

LEARNING FROM MISTAKES

Of course, as your child is working with more and more letters and words, the opportunity for errors will always exist. Yes, it is best that practice is always with the correct letter name or sound. But as your child learns more and more, there are more and more chances that mistakes will be made. When we work with our children, we have the chance to turn mistakes into learning experiences and guide our children to think through the error and correct it themselves. For example, if you ask your child to find the letter *p* and she finds a *q,* find the letter *p* card or draw a *p,* and then ask your child how the *q* is different or what she would have to do to change the *q* into a *p.* Research has shown that pointing out and helping children attend to differences in rotation and orientation of letters such as *b* and *d* can speed their ability to distinguish and accurately identify such letters.[5]

If your child mistakes the /ch/ sound for the /tr/ sound when spelling the word *tree* or *truck,* explain how close he was. Tell him that you can hear how /ch/ and /tr/ can sound an awful lot alike. Take the opportunity to exaggerate the pronunciation of those sounds, and share examples of words that start with each of the sounds. See whether your child can tell you which words start with /ch/ and which with /tr/, and see whether he can come up with words of his own. In other words, don't ever let an error go with "No, that's wrong." Recognize mistakes as teachable moments, and use them to their full advantage.

USING THIS BOOK

The activities in this book are geared primarily toward children in preschool through second grade. Most of the activities are designed for beginning readers but can be adapted to reinforce spelling skills in children as old as ten years. The most crucial piece of equipment for doing *Simon Says . . . "Reading Is Fun"* activities is at least one set of Alphabet Letter Cards, both upper- and lowercase. One set is the minimum, but many games will require two or more sets. The more Alphabet Letter Cards you have, the more flexibility you have. You can either make your own cards or you can order ready-made sets. See appendix C for more information.

Other equipment used for various games and activities includes jump ropes, chalk, hula hoops, balls, boxes, and scooter boards. Each game and activity in the book is preceded by information on the teaching objective, materials, setting, and number of participants needed. While all the materials are probably readily accessible at a school, you may or may not have them around the house. Don't reject an activity just because you don't have the equipment. This is your opportunity to be creative. At our school, the games are always being transformed and altered depending on where we are, who is playing, and what is available. Flexibility is key, and the possibilities are endless.

The charts found in appendices A and B will help you to select games and activities according to the skills you wish to reinforce and the grade level of your child. The grade levels are, of course, approximate. To see whether an activity will accomplish what you wish it to, you will simply have to try it out. If it works, great! If not, it could be for a variety of reasons. A game might be reinforcing a simple concept like letter sounds, but the rules of the game might be too complicated for a younger child. Or perhaps a particular activity just isn't that interesting to your child.

Few of the activities require a lot of setup, so it is easy to move to something new if your first choice doesn't work as planned. The one activity that takes a little time to set up, Alphabet Sea, is worth the effort in that it offers much flexibility. There are literally dozens of things you can do and skills that can be practiced once the "sea" is in place; this activity is an excellent starting place.

WHEN ALL ELSE FAILS, READ!

We believe that the playful qualities of these games and activities will motivate the most reticent of beginning readers. But as much fun as *Simon Says . . . "Reading Is Fun"* can be, we recognize that there are simply days or times when those letters or sounds or words just aren't going to be attended to despite all of our best efforts. This book is full of ideas to engage children when they are having a fidgety day. But there are grouchy days and sleepy days and "I just don't feel like it" days as well. Those are the days to forget about letters and words for a bit and do more of the most important thing of all: read to your child.

Many books are chock-full of suggestions for reading to your child. More and more schools are strongly encouraging adults not only to read to children but to do so in specific ways. Some of the suggestions include pointing to words as they are read, pointing out the title and name of the author of the book, and drawing your child's attention to the left to right progression we use when reading. All of these suggestions are good ones and will help your child to come to understand important concepts about books and reading.

We need not forget, though, that sometimes reading purely for the pleasure of the experience is the most important thing of all. Parent involvement may well be paramount to children's success in school, but assisting your child as she goes about mastering specific skills is not so important that limits of tolerance, yours or hers, are pushed to the point of frustration. Working with your child should enhance the relationship, not risk damaging it.

To be effective in teaching our own children, we must recognize when it's time to drop everything and snuggle up with a good book. Good readers tend to also be those individuals who enjoy reading. Let your child experience reading as pleasurable. Pick books that you enjoy so that in your excitement and enthusiasm your child experiences the joy of reading firsthand. Select books that express your mood or that cheer you up, and explain to your child why you have selected a particular book. If I have been a little snippy or cross with my child, I might pick Robert Munsch's *Love You Forever.* If my child has had a grouchy day, he is sure to relate to *Alexander and the Terrible, Horrible, No Good, Very Bad Day* by Judith Viorst. I love to read Maurice

Sendak's *Where the Wild Things Are,* trying to read a whole page in one breath and roaring where appropriate. And what can be more fun than Dr. Seuss—any Dr. Seuss book at all. So pick a good book, snuggle up tight to your child, and remember, Simon says "Reading is fun!"

NOTES

1. Marilyn Jager Adams, *Beginning to Read* (Cambridge, Mass.: MIT Press, 1994), 357.

2. Adams, *Beginning to Read,* 361.

3. G. L. Bond and R. Dykstra, "The Cooperative Research Program in First Grade Instruction," *Reading Research Quarterly* 5: 5–141 (1967). Quoted in Adams, *Beginning to Read,* 61.

4. Wendy Cheney and Judith Cohen, *Focus on Phonics: Assessment and Instruction* (Bothell, Wash.: Wright Publishing/ McGraw-Hill, 1999), 180.

5. Adams, *Beginning to Read,* 349.

CHAPTER 4

Skills Addressed in This Book

When one stops to think about all the skills involved in learning to read, it is a marvel that so many children learn to read as early as they do. The games and activities in this book are designed to reinforce only some of the skills necessary to send children on their way to mastery of this complex process. The majority of the activities focus on letter identification skills.

The ability to name letters and their corresponding sounds is a cognitively complex task that involves many subskills. Adams points out that letters "were not designed with an eye toward visual distinctiveness or memorability. They are graphically abstract, having no prior iconic significance."[1] Yet we educators expect young children to learn their letters quickly and efficiently!

To achieve fluency with letter and sound identification tasks, children need lots of opportunities to practice. As we have mentioned in earlier chapters, unless the child is attending and engaged, there is little possibility for learning. Anyone who has worked with young children knows that keeping them focused on any one thing for very long is no easy task. The games and activities on the pages to follow are designed to be fast moving, varied, and fun. To adults, they may look simplistic and repetitive. Indeed, they are repetitive in that many of the activities allow for practice of the exact same skills. Having had firsthand experience working with young, fidgety children who are struggling to learn letters, we know that these activities are fun and playful for the children, and thus they keep them engaged in the letter practice they need. We also know that the fun and variety of the games and activities will keep older and more capable students engaged as long as the skills addressed for those students are at their level. We hope you will use *Simon Says . . . "Reading Is Fun!"* with all of the children you work with, to make the challenges involved in learning to read a bit more fun and playful.

Preceding the description of each game or activity you will find a listing of the specific skills that can be reinforced in that context. Because we might understand or label a skill somewhat differently from our readers, we will use this chapter to explain just how we are conceptualizing the skills and the tasks. Following those explanations, we will take the opportunity to briefly define and explain some of the terms we use when discussing the games and activities.

LETTER IDENTIFICATION SKILLS

Letter Matching

Before children can be expected to name letters, one needs to be certain that they can discriminate between them. Matching activities involve showing and naming a specific letter and then having students find that letter. A more sophisticated type of matching involves pairing uppercase letters with their lowercase versions.

Letter Recognition

Most children will be able to recognize a named letter before they themselves can name it. Think of the difference between a test that presents a list of possible answers and one that asks you to recall the correct answer without any cues. Few would disagree that a test that allows us to recognize the right answer is the easier one. Letter recognition activities involve calling out a letter name and having the child select that particular letter from an assortment of Alphabet Letter Cards.

Letter Naming

Naming letters is the most cognitively complex of the letter identification skills. To name a letter, the child must have correctly encoded its shape in her memory, associated that particular letter shape with its specific name, and be able to quickly retrieve that name upon seeing the letter shape. When you consider that uppercase letters and their lowercase versions are called by the same name, you can see how tricky this task really is. This skill will develop more readily if children are given plenty of practice with matching and recognition activities. Letter-naming activities involve you or the student selecting a letter and then asking the child to name that letter.

Sound Identification

While fluent letter-naming skills are a well-established early indicator of later reading proficiency,[2] reading is dependent on one's ability to recall and produce letter sounds quickly and efficiently. Just as with letter identification, the ability to link and recall the sound or sounds connected to individual letters involves subskills and stages.

Sound Matching

Before children can identify letter sounds children, they need to be able to discriminate auditorily among those sounds. It can also be argued that they must be able to produce those sounds as well. Sound-matching activities can consist of having the child produce a given letter sound once it is provided for him. For example, "*B* says /b/. What sound does *B* make?" Or, sound-matching activities could consist of having the child tell you a word that starts with a particular sound.

Sound Recognition

Sound recognition activities involve supplying the student with a letter sound and then having him find the letter or letters that makes that sound. It is a good idea to have the children tell you the letter that corresponds to the sound before they search for it. Having them say the letter name aloud will serve as an additional memory cue. This approach is also helpful because it can alert you to the misperception of or confusion between certain sounds. For example, it is not at all uncommon for young students to respond, "*B*," when you make the /p/ sound.

Sound Naming

Perhaps we should refer to sound naming as sound production, as what we are asking students to do is to produce a given sound. Nonetheless, sound naming has become the term we use to refer to two types of activities. The easier of the two consists of saying a letter and asking for its sound. Because you have provided the letter name, which often provides a clue as to its sound, it is not as difficult as the second type of sound-naming activity. The more difficult activity involves showing the student a particular letter shape and having her produce its sound. Fluency with this more difficult skill is, of course, absolutely essential to becoming a reader.

LETTER-MAKING SKILLS

Letter Copying

Letter-copying activities consist of showing students a letter shape and having them copy that shape. Letter copying can be done with a variety of materials and in a variety of ways. Often, we have the students use chalk or paper and pencils, but painting letters with paint or with water (on a dark surface) are also options. Other ways of copying include making letter shapes with jump ropes or with the children's own bodies. Children also love to "drive" letter shapes with scooter boards.

Letter Making

Letter formation activities ask the child to make or write a letter but without the benefit of seeing the letter shape to copy. Letter-making activities can involve the same variety of mediums as letter-copying tasks.

WORD-MAKING SKILLS

Word Copying

Word-copying activities are those where the children are given word cards and instructed to find the Alphabet Letter Cards needed to make the word. Or, they may be directed to write the word using chalk or jump ropes.

Word Spelling

Spelling tasks are, of course, any activities in which the students are given a word orally and are then expected to spell out the word with Alphabet Letter Cards, jump ropes, paint and brushes, chalk, and so forth.

Word Creation

This skill is practiced during those activities in which the students are provided with an assortment of Alphabet Letter Cards and then directed to make as many words as they can think of. Activities in which each child is assigned a letter sound or name and children work together to configure themselves into a word are also practicing this skill.

PHONOLOGICAL SKILLS

The English language, like all languages, is made up of a variety of sounds. *Phonological awareness* is the ability to identify and manipulate language sounds. At the most basic level, phonological awareness simply involves an ear for language demonstrated, for example, by a familiarity with nursery rhymes. At its most complex level, it is an ability to break words into their individual phonemes and then add and delete phonemes to create new words. While research shows that phonological and phonemic awareness develop as the ability to read develops, this awareness of language sounds is also an early predictor of later reading proficiency.[3]

Phonological and phonemic skills are at the auditory level. That is, children are listening to the sounds of words, not reading them. So, while the sound-matching activities described earlier could be listed in this section, the sound recognition and sound-naming activities, which involve matching sounds to letter shapes, would not necessarily fit in this category. Nonetheless, both phonemic and phonic (connecting sounds to letters) skills are essential to becoming a reader.[4] Thus, you will find activities in this book that involve both types of skills.

Rhyming

Rhyming activities are, of course, those activities that ask the students to create or recognize words that rhyme.

Sentence Segmentation

Before children can begin to hear and understand that words are made up of individual sounds, they must understand what words are and that words make up sentences. Sentence segmentation activities are those that have children break sentences down into words by clapping, jumping, or even literally cutting sentence strips into words. Sentence segmentation activities are especially appropriate for preschool and beginning kindergarten-age students.

Syllable Segmentation

As you might already expect, *syllable segmentation* is when individual words are broken down into the separate syllables. As with sentence segmentation, these activities require children to break words down into syllables by jumping and clapping.

Phonemic Blending

Phonemic-blending activities are those in which the students must blend individual sounds into words. Typically, activities that require blending will occur at the phonic level; students will be looking at a word they have created and sounding it out. However, when an individual child is not yet working at this level, the teacher or other adult can adapt such an activity to develop phonemic-blending skills. Specifically, if the child has made the word *bat* with his Alphabet Letter Cards but cannot read that word, the individual working with that students makes the individual letter sounds /b/, /a/, /t/ and allows the student to blend those sounds into the word *bat*.

Phoneme Segmentation

This is the most sophisticated of phonological skills. With this type of segmentation, words are broken down even further so that each word or syllable in a word is broken into its individual phonemes. For example, the word *cat* becomes /c/, /a/, /t/. Again, phonemic segmentation activities involve clapping, jumping, or hopping the individual sounds.

OTHER SKILLS

Alphabetic Sequencing Activities

Alphabetic-sequencing activities, as you might expect, are any activities that require the students to arrange their Alphabet Letter Cards or written or spoken letters in alphabetic sequence.

Body Part Identification Activities

These activities are also rather self-explanatory. They are games that require students to identify or locate various parts of their own bodies. While playing games like Simon Says, it is easy to remember to ask children to wave their arm or lift their leg, but don't forget those more obscure parts like chins and shins and heels.

Directionality Activities

Directionality activities are those that teach and reinforce spatial positioning concepts. These activities are often brief and can be done quickly between other games or activities, or they can fill the time at the beginning or end of an instructional period. When teaching directionality terms to younger children or to children who seem to be very kinesthetic in their approach to learning, you may want to have them position their own body before they try to position objects in the room. For example, ask them to "Stand next to something green" before you ask them to "Put your scooter board next to something green."

DEFINITION OF TERMS

In this section, we define or explain some of the terms that show up in the pages to follow. Some are well known from the reading literature. Some are things you may only find in this book because they are the names we have assigned to some activity or thing. Other terms describe the type of materials we might use. In listing the terms, we have tried to keep related terms together and have listed real terms before our made-up ones.

Phoneme

A *phoneme* is the smallest unit of sound in a language. Some phonemes consist of a single-letter sound, but others are represented by two or more letters. Words are made up of individual phonemes. The English language contains forty-four phonemes.

Onset

In words and syllables, any consonants that precede the vowel make up the onset in that word. Of course, words beginning with vowels would not have an onset.[5]

Rime

In words and syllables, the *rime* is made up of the vowel and all of the consonants following it. While *rime* is not to be confused with *rhyme,* it is the part of words that causes them to rhyme. For example, in the word *stitch, -itch* is the rime. The rime *-itch* is also the part of *stitch* that makes it rhyme with *witch*.[6]

Alphabet Sea

An Alphabet Sea is created when numerous sets of Alphabet Letter Cards are spread over a large area. We typically use the school's gym, and because we have accumulated many sets of letters, our "sea" is quite large. You can create a smaller sea in a classroom or other space. Also, depending on the age and ability level of the children you are working with, your sea can include Word Cards as well as Alphabet Letter Cards.

Alphabet Letter Cards

Alphabet Letter Cards are essential equipment for the majority of *Simon Says . . . "Reading Is Fun!"* activities. Mostly, we use small cards that are approximately four inches by six inches. You can find more information on how to make your own Alphabet Letter Cards in appendix C.

Word Cards

Word Cards are simply rectangular pieces of oak tag or construction paper with words written on them. We like to use lots of colors for our cards, letters, and words to make them more visually appealing. You can find suggestions for the types of words to use in appendices C.

Wall Letters

Wall Letters are large letters, about thirty-six inches high, that we cut out of various colors of butcher paper. The letters hang on the wall of the gym and are used for some of the activities. If you have the space available, they are useful and yet another visual reminder of letter shapes for your students. However, it is possible to do most of the activities in this book without making these giant letters.

Directionality

When we talk about directionality, we are referring to those words that help us to understand the relative position of things. A list of directionality words can be found in appendix D.

Scooter Boards

While physical educators may know just what we mean by a scooter board, the rest of our readers may be a bit puzzled. *Scooter boards* are the four-wheeled skateboard equivalent used in physical education classes. Typically, they are used in K–2 programs to work on muscular strength, directionality, and other objectives. Kids love them, but unlike with skateboards, students may not stand on them. Any other position (kneeling, sitting, lying) is possible while maneuvering a scooter board.

Driving

In quite a few activities, you will note that students are directed to "drive" their letters or words. What we mean by this is that they will mount their scooter board and roll along the floor as if they are driving on a letter-shaped track or road. This is a way for the children to get a feel for the way the letter shape is formed.

Lummi Sticks

Again, lummi sticks are equipment familiar to physical educators and music teachers as well, but not necessarily to the rest of us. These sticks are the wooden sticks used in physical education and music classes to work on rhythm skills. Usually, each student has a pair of sticks, one for each hand, and uses them to follow along in a coordinated rhythmical routine (or creates a routine alone or with a partner).

H Brothers

H Brothers is the term used by Project Read[7] to introduce the digraphs /wh/, /ch/, /th/, and /sh/. You might want to consider making H brother cards along with your Alphabet Letter and Word Cards.

NOTES

1. Marilyn Jager Adams, *Beginning to Read* (Cambridge, Mass.: MIT Press, 1994), 346–47.
2. J. S. Chall, *Learning to Read: The Great Debate,* updated ed. (New York: McGraw-Hill, 1983), quoted in Adams, *Beginning to Read,* 61.
3. Adams, *Beginning to Read,* 55–91.
4. P. E. Bryant and L. Bradley, "Why Children Sometimes Write Words They Do Not Read," in *Cognitive Processes in Spelling,* ed. U. Frith (New York: Academic Press, 1980), quoted in Adams, *Beginning to Read,* 304.
5. Adams, *Beginning to Read,* 308.
6. Adams, *Beginning to Read,* 308.
7. Victoria E. Greene and Mary Lee Enfield, *Phonology Guide, Project Read* (Bloomington, Minn.: Language Circle Enterprises, 1991), 11:1.

CHAPTER 5

Games and Activities

This chapter describes activities and games listed by grade level, beginning at the lower level. Keep in mind that the recommended grade level is only a suggestion as you may find that some activities or games target a different age level than the one listed. In addition, you may find that, with a little adapting, your activity or game will reach even more than the grade levels targeted.

Some of the games can be altered to become more cooperative than competitive, and some activities altered to be more gamelike. The key is to meet the needs of the kinesthetic learners while teaching the early literacy skills necessary to read. Have fun!

Alphabet Sea

> **Objectives:** Alphabetic Sequencing, Letter Copying, Letter Match-
> ing, Letter Recognition, Letter Naming, Sound Matching, Sound
> Recognition, Sound Naming, Word Creation, Word Copying,
> Word Spelling, and Word Matching
> **Equipment:** Alphabet Letter Cards
> **Area:** Classroom, Gymnasium, or Outdoors
> **Number of Participants:** 1+
> **Grades:** Pre-K–2

The "Alphabet Sea" is what we call it when we scatter alphabet letter
cards all over the gym floor. This idea came from *Movement Activities
for the Young Child.*[1] Most of the activities require that the Alphabet Letter Cards are face up, so that the students are able to see the letters on
each card. Usually we scatter the cards in an area in the center of the gym
so that the perimeter may be used for other activities. Placing the cards
yourself can be time-consuming if you are using several alphabet sets,
but the time spent is worth it.

Countless activities and games are possible once you have created
your Alphabet Sea. We have listed lots of ideas here and are sure you
will think of many more on your own. Our suggestions are geared primarily to the kindergarten and first grade students we have worked with
who were still developing their letter identification skills and knowledge of letter sounds. With older students, you might want to have them
use the Alphabet Sea to practice their spelling words. With younger students, you might want to have them find matching sets, or you could
show a particular letter and have the children find one that matches. In
addition to varying the task, you can always vary the movement
through the Alphabet Sea. You could instruct the children to run, hop,
skip, "swim," or "surf" (on scooter boards) as they search for letters.
Here are some suggested activities:

1. Have students search for a letter that is in their favorite color.
2. Have students search for a letter that is in their first name.
3. Have students search for a letter that is in their middle name.

4. Have students search for a letter that is in their last name.
5. Have students search for a letter that is curvy.
6. Have students search for a letter that looks like a number.
7. Have students search for a letter that is a vowel.
8. Have students search for a letter that is a consonant.
9. Have students search for a letter that they can identify and tell its name.
10. Have students search for a letter for which they can make the sound.
11. Have students search for a letter that they can identify and make the sound.

After one or more of these directives have been given, add:

1. Can you tell me the name of that letter?
2. Can you tell your neighbor the name of that letter?
3. Can you make the sound of that letter?
4. Can you make that letter with your body?
5. Can you make that letter using a jump rope?
6. Can you write that letter with chalk?
7. Can you drive that letter with your scooter board?
8. Can you "write" that letter using a lummi stick? (Make sure if the lummi sticks are painted that they will not mark the floor.)
9. Can you tell me a word that has that letter/sound in it?

Or try these directives:

1. Can you find the first letter in your first name?
2. Can you find the second letter in your first name?
3. Can you find the third letter in your first name?
4. Can you find the first letter in your last name?
5. Can you find the second letter in your last name?
6. Can you find the third letter in your last name?

Sometimes the students will want to pick up the letters and carry them around with them as they locate the next letter needed. If there are plenty of letters, this is fine; otherwise, they will need to work with the letter where they find it, let it stay there, and move on to the next letter. Remind the students they are not to fold, bend, (or chew) the Alphabet Letter Cards, so that the cards last longer and look nicer.

Directionality is important, so these directives might be added along with letter identification:

1. Can you sit/stand/lay on top of the letter?
2. Can you sit/stand/lie behind the letter?
3. Can you sit/stand/lie in front of the letter?
4. Can you sit/stand/lie beside the letter?
5. Can you stand over the letter?
6. Can you sit/stand/lie under the letter?
7. Can you sit near a *C*?
8. Can you sit far away from all of the letters?
9. Can you get very close to the letter without touching it?
10. How far away can you stand from the first letter in your first name?

As previously mentioned, all of these activities involve the alphabet letters remaining in the "sea"—that is, scattered around the floor for use in further activity. There are, of course, numerous activities that could involve collecting the letters, such as spelling practice, "writing" their names or sight words, collecting and sequencing an entire alphabet, and matching upper- and lowercase letters. Any activity involving the collecting of cards could become part of the cleanup process.

We have never cleaned up the cards ourselves, as lots of activities can involve the students' picking up the cards. Have students clean up by picking up as much "treasure" as they possibly can, and then have them count their loot. Have students clean up by letter, with students searching and collecting the letter(s) of their choice or yours. Have students collect letters by letter or card color. Have students collect all the letters they can find that are in their own name. Students may collect cards for cleanup by simply picking them up and holding onto them or by using a bucket or box. They can travel about the room "driving" a scooter board, or they could be directed to run, skip, or hop as they collect cards. Plan that cleanup may be time-consuming if counting is involved, if all the letters are still remaining on the floor or if it is one of the initial times used for activity and the novelty has yet to wear off.

Identify a Letter

> **Objectives:** Letter Matching, Letter Recognition, Letter Naming, Sound Recognition, and Sound Naming
> **Equipment:** Large Alphabet Cutouts, Alphabet Letter Cards, and Wall Letters
> **Area:** Classroom, Hallway, Gymnasium, or Outdoors
> **Number of Participants:** 1+
> **Grades:** Pre-K–2

Using butcher paper, create large letters about thirty-six to forty-eight inches high. Begin with the letters being taught in the classroom and add on, as the teacher does. For example, if the teacher is starting with the letters *R, T, A, C,* and *S,* then those are the only letters displayed on the gym walls. Gradually, the alphabet unfolds as time moves along. The letters taped onto the wall serve two purposes: they are used for games such as this one, and they can be used to refer to a specific letter that a student may be struggling with, when playing a different game or activity. The activity is really a list of "Can you . . . ?" questions, limited only by your imagination. Here is a sample list to get you started:

> Can you find the letter *T*?
> Can you find the vowel?
> Can you find a consonant?
> Can you find the letter that matches this sound? (Make the sound of the letter you want students to find.)
> Can you find this letter? (Flash a larger version of the Alphabet Letter Cards for the students to see, and then match with your wall letters.)
> Can you find the pink letter? Can you find a letter that is in your name?

Once the students have located the letter requested, by standing near it or sitting under it, ask them what letter it is and what sound it makes. As you add different activities and games to challenge the students, the alphabet letters hanging on your gym wall become a reference for the students. For example, you might ask students to "Find the letter *P*." A student having difficulty because he forgot what a *P* looks like can refer to the wall. You might say, "*P* is the color orange; can you find it?" Or, you can ask the student to stand near or under the letter on the wall that she thinks is the letter *P*, and then direct her from that point with the help necessary.

Create a Letter

> **Objectives:** Letter Copying, Letter Naming, and Sound Recognition
> **Equipment:** Lummi Sticks, Bean Bags, Hockey Sticks, and Noodles
>   (foam pool toys)
> **Area:** Classroom, Hallway, Gymnasium, or Outdoors
> **Number of Participants:** 1+
> **Grades:** Pre-K–2

This activity is very simple but uses a variety of equipment. Present a letter in differing formats, asking the students to create the given letter. In many of the activities and games in this book, we have pointed out some alternative ways to create, recall, and practice letters and their matching sounds. Jump Rope Roundup makes use of "writing" with jump ropes. Fun with Paintbrushes makes use of "writing" with paintbrush and water. Speed Racer does the same with scooter boards. This activity is really the catchall for all the other ways in which students can practice their letters, sounds, and even words. Using whatever equipment is handy, have students "write" with anything that excites and engages them. Boxes, yarn, balls—anything will work!

You might say, "Make the letter *M*." You could also make the sound of the letter—for example, "Make the letter that matches /m/." Sometimes, simply showing a large flash card with an alphabet letter on it is challenging enough for the students to create.

Jumping Jellybeans . . . and Elephants, Too!

> **Objectives:** Syllable Segmentation, Sentence Segmentation, and
>   Phonemic Segmentation
> **Equipment:** Hula Hoops (optional: rubber discs, empty boxes)
> **Area:** Classroom, Gymnasium, or Outdoors
> **Number of Participants:** 1+
> **Grades:** Pre-K–3

The name for this activity refers to Project Read's terminology for one-syllable and multisyllable words. One-syllable words are said to be jellybean words because like jellybeans, the whole word fits into your mouth at once. Elephants, however, are way too big to fit into our mouths. If we wanted to eat an elephant (a proposition sure to emit gleeful "yucks" from young children), we would have to slice it into pieces. Multisyllabic words, like elephants, don't fit into our mouths all at once and have to be "sliced" into syllables.[2] This activity helps children to hear, see, and feel the size of various words as they say, clap, and jump each syllable.

Typically, we have the children use their names for the initial practice with this activity. Using our own name first, we clap the name using one clap for each syllable. We count the claps and then lay out one hula hoop for each syllable we clapped. We then jump into the lined-up hoops, pronouncing each syllable as we jump. The students can be partnered, or they can work alone. When working with a partner, one child can say and clap the word while the other child counts and places the hula hoops in a row.

To reinforce left-to-right progression, we have the children place the hoops in a horizontal line with the first syllable "placed" on the left. This means we will jump into the first hoop on left and continue down the line.

This activity can quickly become a competition to see who can think of the word with the most syllables. There are countless ways to extend and modify this activity. Sometimes we have the students get Alphabet Letter Cards and spell each syllable inside the hoop. This works best with their names or other words they can already easily spell. You may want to ask the children to spell their name or a word with the letter cards first and then determine which letters make up which syllable.

With younger children, you may want to begin with the easier task of segmenting the words in a sentence. Instead of clapping syllables in a word, have the students count and clap the number of words in a sentence. As described earlier, children will lay out the correct number of hula hoops and jump their sentence.

This activity can also be adapted and used for breaking words into individual phonemes. Use something smaller than hula hoops when breaking words into phonemes, to help students understand that phonemes are the smallest sound parts in words. In our gym, for example, we have some pink rubber discs. The smaller discs are for phonemes, while the hula hoops are for syllables. Our discs are small enough that they can placed inside of the hula hoop but large enough that we can place some letter cards on top. When they are all laid out, the children get a great visual representation of a word broken into all its parts. Instead of hula hoops, empty boxes (shoe boxes or, for bigger fun, packing boxes) can be used to "build words," stacking one box for each word, syllable, or phoneme. Left-to-right progression is not reinforced, but the students will have a great time trying to think of and build very tall sentences or words.

ABC Order

> **Objectives:** Alphabetic Sequencing, Letter Matching, Letter Recognition, Letter Naming, Sound Matching, and Sound Naming
> **Equipment:** Alphabet Letter Cards (Two or more sets may be necessary.)
> **Area:** Classroom, Gymnasium, or Outdoors
> **Number of Participants:** 1+
> **Grades:** K–2

Place one letter of each of the letters of the alphabet in an area, and have students arrange the cards into the correct order. Students may work alone or in pairs or small groups. If desired, you can make the activity competitive by having the various pairs or groups race to beat the clock or one another.

Once the letters are assembled in the correct order, students can tell the name of each letter, the sound of each letter, name the vowels, or state a word that begins with the letter or sound of selected alphabet letters.

Students can write each letter below the letter card, once arranged properly, to practice creating their own alphabet.

Create an Alphabet

> **Objectives:** Alphabetic Sequencing, Letter Copying, Letter Recognition, and Sound Naming
> **Equipment:** Alphabet Letter Cards (two or more sets may be necessary)
> **Area:** Classroom, Gymnasium, or Outdoors
> **Number of Participants:** 1+
> **Grades:** K–2

Place an Alphabet Sea in the area of play. Have students move in the Alphabet Sea, searching for letters needed to create the alphabet in correct order. Students may work alone or in pairs. Once they have found some letters, they may lay them out in the correct order in their work space. Some students will search for all letters before assembling in correct order and may need a bucket or Frisbee to carry their letters to avoid dropping them. Other students may retrieve and place one letter at a time.

You can vary this activity by changing the task to all uppercase or lowercase letters for some students, while others simply need to retrieve the correct letter regardless of case. You can have students write the letter below each card, to practice creating the alphabet on their own. Students who finish early can lay out the alphabet backward.

52 Pickup

> **Objectives:** Alphabetic Sequencing, Letter Matching, Letter Recognition, Letter Naming, Sound Naming, and Word Spelling
> **Equipment:** Alphabet Letter Cards and Word Cards
> **Area:** Classroom, Hallway, Gymnasium, or Outdoors
> **Number of Participants:** 1+
> **Grades:** K–2

This game is just like the card game "52 Pickup." You or the students may toss Alphabet Letter Cards into the air, so they fall haphazardly to the floor. Have students run to a letter of choice, pick it up, and shout (or whisper or draw) the name of the letter. They may add the letter back to the pile of letters or bring it to you. The latter approach makes it easier for assessing what letters are known and which ones still need to be learned.

You can ask students to find a given letter. You can make the sound of a letter and ask students to find the letter that matches the sound. You can show a letter and have a student find a match. You can show the uppercase version of a letter and ask the student to find its lowercase version, and vice versa. You can play the game using Word Cards, with the same type of variations as mentioned.

Sandman

> **Objectives:** Letter Copying, Letter Naming, Sound Matching, Sound Recognition, Sound Naming, Word Copying, Word Spelling, and Word Creation
> **Equipment:** Sandbox or other area with sand and Alphabet Letter Cards
> **Area:** Gymnasium or Outdoors
> **Number of Participants:** 1+
> **Grades:** K–2

Use a sandbox or other large play area where there is sand. Ask students to write the letters of the alphabet in the sand, using their finger, a stick, or even a toy truck or car. This may sound similar to sand writing, a popular tactile activity. However, Sandman is played in a larger area and allows for more whole-body movement. You may give the name of a letter and ask the students to write it, say the sound of a letter and ask them to write it, or show an Alphabet Letter Card and ask them to copy it in the sand. You can tell them to write the upper- or lowercase version of the letter. You might show the uppercase version and ask the student to write the lowercase version. You could show a Word Card and ask the student to write it. You can say a sight word and ask the student to write it. You might write a letter in the sand and have the student tell you the name of it. Take turns by playing a game of guessing the letter. You could have the student draw something that begins with the sound of the letter given.

Jump Rope Roundup

> **Objectives:** Letter Copying, Letter Matching, Letter Naming, Sound
>   Matching, and Sound Naming
> **Equipment:** Jump Ropes (one or more per student), Alphabet Letter
>   Cards, and Word Cards
> **Area:** Classroom, Hallway, Gymnasium, or Outdoors
> **Number of Participants:** 1+
> **Grades:** K–2

Jump Rope Roundup is a simple activity to practice making alphabet letters. You may start by showing the students an Alphabet Letter Card and asking them to create the same letter using their jump rope. Most letters can be made using only one jump rope, but some letters may require more than one. Some students may use their bodies, in addition to the jump rope, to complete a letter. For example, a student might place a rope in a straight line on the floor and lay with her body perpendicular to it to create the letter *T*.

To add variety to this activity, you could say the letter and ask students to make it with their ropes. In this activity, students have to recall the letter to make it. You might make the sound of a letter and have students make the letter that matches the sound.

Be sure that you ask students to tell you the name of the letter they have created and tell what sound it makes, if they can do so. You might also ask the students if they can say a word that begins with that letter. You can use this activity to learn new letters or to review letters and sounds. Students may help each other, as needed.

Creating words with the jump ropes is another activity that students enjoy. With an ample supply of jump ropes on hand, there is no limit to what students can "write." Give each student a Word Card and plenty of ropes and have them "write" the word. After is it "written," ask them to tell you what word they wrote, how to spell it, and maybe even to use the word in a sentence. Once they have done so, with or without some help from you, give them a new Word Card and start again.

Some students may be ready to form sentences with words they "write" on their own or with help from the words you give them from the Word Cards.

Fun with Chalk

> **Objectives:** Letter Copying, Letter Recognition, Letter Naming, Sound Recognition, Sound Matching, Word Copying, and Word Spelling
>
> **Equipment:** Chalk, Alphabet Letter Cards, and Word Cards
> **Area:** Outdoors
> **Number of Participants:** 1+
> **Grades:** K–2

Children love to write and draw with chalk, so this is a great way to stimulate writing with something colorful and different. This activity is enacted primarily on the playground in warm weather, but it can be done indoors, on the gym or cafeteria floor, which can easily be mopped after the activity. It can also be done in a hallway, using butcher paper or cardboard. Some floors will not mop up easily after written and drawn with chalk; test a small area first to see if this is something that can be done in your environment. The sidewalk chalk that comes with a variety of colors and is easier for small hands to grasp is a favorite, but even the chalkboard chalk used by the teacher is a treat in many classrooms!

Say the name of a letter and have students write the letter with chalk. You can have the student tell the sound of the letter, once he has written with chalk, or you could say the sound of a letter and have the students write the letter that matches it. You might show the uppercase version of a letter and have the students write the lowercase version of it, and vice versa.

You could have students tell the name of something that begins with the sound of the letter they have written. Students might also draw a picture of something that begins with the sound of the letter they have written.

Students can also write words using their chalk. You can give them a Word Card and ask them to write the word and then tell the word they have written. You can say a word and have them write it; then check their own work with use of a Word Card. You can have students write their spelling words, for practice, rather than repeating aloud or writing with pencil.

Speed Racer

>**Objectives:** Letter Copying, Sound Recognition, Word Spelling, and
>   Directionality Terms
>**Equipment:** One Scooter Board per Student, Alphabet Letter Cards,
>   and Word Cards
>**Area:** Gymnasium or Outdoors
>**Number of Participants:** 1+
>**Grades:** K–2

Speed Racer is an activity for both working on letters and expending
energy. Use this activity for a quick release of energy when you want
to provide some variety in the kinesthetic realm, but do not worry about
assessing their letter identification. Review the safety rules for scooter
boards, and then get started!

The students "write" an alphabet letter by driving their scooter
board. Some students might sit or lay on the scooter board; others
might run behind, carefully gripping the board as though it is a steering
wheel. A demonstration might be necessary the first time you offer this
activity. With some students it may be helpful to explain that it is like
having paint on the wheels of the scooter board. The student will
"paint" the letter on the floor by driving the scooter board. You might
ask students to simply make the letter or specify upper- or lowercase,
or both. You can make the sound of a letter and have students drive the
letter that matches it. Students may drive their names or words from
Word Cards.

To practice directionality terms, tell the students to drive around
something black, near a curvy line, counterclockwise, or to the left of
the teacher. Word Cards can also be created giving students practice on
both reading and learning the directionality concepts.

Fun with Paintbrushes

> **Objectives:** Letter Copying, Letter Naming, Sound Recognition, Sound Matching, Word Copying, and Word Spelling
> **Equipment:** Paintbrush, Container of Water, Alphabet Letter Cards, and Word Cards
> **Area:** Outdoors
> **Number of Participants:** 1+
> **Grades:** K–2

Children love to paint, so this is a great way to stimulate writing with a unique tool, the paintbrush. This is primarily a warm-weather playground activity, but it can also be done indoors, on floors such as a gym or cafeteria, which can easily be mopped after the activity. It can also be done in a hallway, using butcher paper or cardboard. The only concern is that when using water indoors on the floor, the surface gets slippery and can be dangerous; use caution.

Give the name of a letter and have students paint the letter using water. You can have the student tell the sound of the letter, once they have painted it, or you could say the sound of a letter and have the students paint the letter that matches it. You could show the uppercase version of a letter and have the students paint the lowercase version of it, and vice versa.

You might have students tell the name of something that begins with the sound of the letter they have painted. You could have students paint a picture of something that begins with the sound of the letter they have painted.

Students can also paint sight words or spelling words. Give students a Word Card and ask them to paint the word and then tell the word they have painted. You could say a word and have them paint it; then check their work with use of a Word Card. You might have students paint their spelling words, for practice, rather than repeating aloud or writing with pencil.

Students would love to use paint, too, for this activity. Butcher paper, paints, finger paints, large brushes, and sponges would make a fun break in the routine of desk work.

Twist and Shout

> **Objectives:** Letter Copying, Letter Naming, Sound Matching, Sound Recognition, Sound Naming, Word Copying, and Word Spelling
> **Equipment:** Twist Ties (for baggies, trash bags, etc.), Alphabet Letter Cards, and Word Cards
> **Area:** Classroom, Hallway, Gymnasium, or Outdoors
> **Number of Participants:** 1+
> **Grades:** K–2

This is an activity that can make use of all the extra twist ties that are sitting in drawers at home. You can also use pipe cleaners, but they would have to be purchased. With the twist ties, the activity is free!

Give the students an Alphabet Letter Card, and have them create the letter using twist ties. The students can then shout or tell the sound of the letter, write it, trace around the twist tie to write it, and shout or tell something that begins with the sound of that letter. You could give the students the sound of a letter and ask them to make the letter that matches the sound. You might give the uppercase version of a letter and ask them to make the lowercase version, and vice versa.

You can use the twist ties over and over, or use new ones for each letter formed. Once students have created a number of letters, have them begin to form words, from memory or with the help of Word Cards. Those students who already know their letters can begin making words right away, and then use the words to build sentences. They can practice their spelling words by making them. The twist ties can be stapled onto construction paper or bulletin boards for demonstration or kept for use in the same or similar activity later.

Read and Run

> **Objectives:** Alphabetic Sequencing, Letter Recognition, Letter Naming, and Sound Naming
>
> **Equipment:** Alphabet Letter Cards (two or more sets may be necessary), Word Cards, and Hula Hoop, Box, or Bucket (for each student)
>
> **Area:** Classroom, Gymnasium, or Outdoors
>
> **Number of Participants:** 1+
>
> **Grades:** K–5

This activity can be used in a variety of ways. For example, we have used it as a means of assessment of letter recognition for kindergarten students. Place an Alphabet Sea with upper- and/or lowercase letters about the room. Have a bucket, box, or hula hoop for all children playing the game, where they are to deposit their letters. To play the game, students run around the area, picking up one letter at a time. The student brings the letter to the teacher and may tell the name of the letter and/or the sound of that letter. Further, the student may tell whether it is upper- or lowercase. Each letter that the student identifies correctly is deposited in the bucket, box, or hula hoop. Then, the student returns to running, skipping, hopping, jumping, rolling, and so forth, around the Alphabet Sea, in search of the next letter, which they have chosen by letter, color, or placement. At the end of the activity, you can identify all letters known by the student by sorting through their bucket, box, or hula hoop. This activity can also be used with words, rather than letters. Place Word Cards in the Alphabet Sea, in addition to the Alphabet Letter Cards. Students who are working on sight words can be searching for them, while students still learning letters will be working at their level. Spelling words can be added to the Alphabet Sea, too!

Tracing with Chalk

> **Objectives:** Letter Copying, Letter Naming, Letter Recognition, Sound Matching, and Sound Recognition
> **Equipment:** Jump Ropes and Chalk
> **Area:** Gymnasium or Outdoors
> **Number of Participants:** 1+
> **Grades:** K–5

Give each student a jump rope and a piece of chalk. Tell or show students a letter that they are to create using their ropes. You might give the sound of a letter and ask the students to create the letter that matches it. After the students create the letter with the rope, ask them to trace it with chalk. Next, they should be able to remove the rope and see the letter formed. Have them name the letter they have made and make its sound. Also, have students tell a word that starts with that letter.

Connect the Dots

Objectives: Alphabetic Sequencing, Letter Recognition, Letter Naming, and Sound Naming
Equipment: Alphabet Letter Cards and Chalk
Area: Gymnasium or Outdoors
Number of Participants: 1+
Grades: K–5

Place an Alphabet Sea in the play area. The task is for the student to draw a line connecting the alphabet letters in the correct order. So, a student begins by locating the letter *A,* then finding *B* and drawing a line from the *A* to the *B,* then moving onto the *C,* and so forth, until the entire alphabet has been found and connected.

Students may work in pairs, in which one student does the drawing of the line and the other partner scouts ahead for the upcoming letter. When possible, you might want to give each student or pair a different color piece of chalk so they don't confuse their paths. When all are finished, the students can go back and "walk" their alphabet path.

Wash Line

> **Objectives:** Letter Matching, Letter Recognition, Letter Naming, Sound Recognition, Word Copying, and Word Spelling
> **Equipment:** Wash Line, Clothespins, Alphabet Letter Cards, and Word Cards
> **Area:** Classroom, Gymnasium, or Outdoors
> **Number of Participants:** 1+
> **Grades:** K–5

Place an Alphabet Sea in the play area. Hang a wash line somewhere in the play area that is long enough for students to hang Alphabet Letter Cards onto; some play spaces may require a few shorter ropes rather than one that is very long. Be sure that the line is at the children's height, so that they can easily reach it. Next, tell students what letter to find, show them the letter to find, or give the sound of the letter to find. Once found, students should get a clothespin and hang it on the line. Repeat, as the students are interested. You might individualize the activity by having students search for the letters they are struggling with, or you may have the entire group searching for the same letters.

An extension of this game is to give students a Word Card. Each student enters the Alphabet Sea and collects the necessary letters to form that word. Next, the students hang the letters in the correct order on the line using the clothespins provided. Ask students to tell what letters make up that word, the sounds of those letters, and the word by name, if they know it.

Body Cutouts

> **Objectives:** Letter Copying, Letter Naming, and Word Spelling
> **Equipment:** Butcher Paper, Scissors, and Pencils or Crayons
> **Area:** Classroom, Hallway, Gymnasium, or Outdoors
> **Number of Participants:** 1+
> **Grades:** K–5

Tear off large pieces of butcher paper from a roll, so that a student could lie completely on top of it. If possible, use lighter-colored paper, as the students will be tracing on it and should be able to see where their pencil lines have marked. Students work in pairs. Each pair of students needs a crayon or pencil, two pairs of scissors, and a few sheets of butcher paper.

One student selects a letter to make with his or her body by lying on top of the sheet of butcher paper. The student's partner should trace the letter, around the partner's body, with pencil or crayon. Have students switch roles, and then each cut out the letter they have formed. If time permits, have students create numerous large letters. You can plan the event so that the students make the entire alphabet. Hang the letters in the gym or hallways or other place for display; these are what we call the Wall Letters. Perhaps the students can make all the letters in their first name or their initials. Perhaps you can tell each student what letter to create, and together, all of the letters will form to make a word, which they can work cooperatively to unscramble.

Mystery Writer

> **Objectives:** Letter Copying, Letter Naming, Sound Recognition, and Word Copying
> **Equipment:** Alphabet Letter Cards
> **Area:** Classroom, Hallway, Gymnasium, or Outdoors
> **Number of Participants:** 2+
> **Grades:** K–5

Each student has a partner. One partner selects an Alphabet Letter Card from the box and "writes" that letter on his or her partner's back using a finger. The partner tries to guess what letter was drawn. If the student is unable to guess, the mystery writer may give a clue by telling what sound that letter makes. The mystery writer can also write the lower-case version of that letter if the partner has difficulty guessing the uppercase, or vice versa. Once the partner guesses the correct letter, the pair should switch roles. This activity is most effective if you tailor it to the particular needs of each child. Choose partners ahead of time, and give each pair a bucket or box of letters selected just for them. A mix of letters that have already been mastered plus a few that have recently been introduced works best.

Once, while playing this game, some students said, "Hey, can we use words?" These students were bored of guessing letters and wanted to be challenged. So, they selected Word Cards instead of Alphabet Letter Cards and wrote the word on their partners' backs.

Puzzles

Objectives: Letter Recognition, Sound Naming, Word Creation, and
Phonemic Blending
Equipment: Alphabet Letter Cards
Area: Classroom, Gymnasium, Hallway, or Outdoors
Number of Participants: 3+
Grades: K–5

Give each student an Alphabet Letter Card. The students are to find
other students with whom they may join to form a word. This game can
be played as an addition to the Barnyard Game, in which students make
the sound of the letter on their card, rather than showing or telling the
letter on the card. It may be helpful to have a few students with *S* letters in the group, to allow students to make a word plural when unable
to form a word of their own. Once a group of students has formed a
word, you can have a student from another group listen to each letter
sound as the individual students make them and blend the sounds into
the word the group has created.

Group Word Formation

> **Objectives:** Word Copying and Word Spelling
> **Equipment:** Word Cards
> **Area:** Classroom, Gymnasium, or Outdoors
> **Number of Participants:** 3+
> **Grades:** 1–5

Place students in groups of three, four, or five depending on the size of the words you select. Give each group a Word Card, or give them a word they are to spell. Students are to create that word, using their bodies to make the letters. If a group has extra players, some letters can be formed with two people, or punctuation can be added such as a period or exclamation point. Finally, if a group has more players than the word requires, one or two players can be designated "teacher" and help to be sure the letters are correct and in the proper order.

As students become adept with this game, you can build to sentences by having each group form a particular word given in a sentence. Again, extra students can play "teacher" by making sure words are spelled correctly and placed in the proper order for the sentence given.

Word Scramble

> **Objectives:** Word Creation, Word Spelling, Letter Copying, and Rhyming
>
> **Equipment:** Alphabet Letter Cards (two or more sets may be necessary), Pencils and Paper or Chalk, Buckets or Boxes (optional: jump ropes, scooter boards)
>
> **Area:** Classroom, Gymnasium, or Outdoors
>
> **Number of Participants:** 1+
>
> **Grades:** 1–5

For this activity, students can work by themselves or in pairs. If you do choose to have students working together, it may be a good idea to pair students with fewer skills with those who have more. Each student or pair of students is given a bucket or box filled with a variety of Alphabet Letter Cards. The students are then directed to create as many words as they can with their cards.

Have the children show you each word as they create them, or they can leave the word in place and move on without showing you. In the gym, we allow the students to write the word they create with chalk right on the floor. That way, they can reuse their letters to create new words. If chalk on the floor is not an option, you can provide paper and pencils, or you could have them paint their words on butcher paper. Other ideas include having the students "write" their words with jump ropes or "drive" their words on a scooter board.

Some students prefer to keep their Alphabet Letter Card words intact rather than or in addition to writing them. When this happens, they will likely run out of cards or at least run out of certain letters. Borrowing or swapping letters from other students is fine. In fact, sometimes this exchange between students leads to new ideas. When children choose not to copy their words with chalk or pencil, you will have to decide just what your objective is and how essential the writing practice is for a particular student.

This activity can be made more challenging for older or more skilled students by giving them specific parameters for the words they create. For example, you might want to specify that the words all start or end with a particular letter. Or, you may want to specify that all the words belong to a specific category (animals, places, things, etc.). Another possibility is having the children create sets of rhyming words.

Find It

> **Objectives:** Letter Matching, Letter Recognition, Sound Recognition, and Directionality Terms
> **Equipment:** None
> **Area:** Classroom, Hallway, Gymnasium, or Outdoors
> **Number of Participants:** 1+
> **Grades:** Pre-K–5

Find It is a game you may use with kindergarten and first grade students in the beginning of the year to orient them to the gym. The game is also helpful when you are playing in a new environment, such as the cafeteria, soccer field, or large-group instruction rooms at our school, for the same purpose. This game can be found in *Follow Me Too*, a book by Marianne Torbert.[3] Tell the students to "Find something blue and touch it." Students respond by doing just that, touching something blue, whether the blue item is on their person, part of a sign or the wall, or on things found within the surroundings. You may also mention before the game begins that, if the students find something blue that is out of their reach, they may point to it instead. Other examples include "Find something made of wood and touch it," "Find something round and touch it," or "Find a line that is black and touch it."

Once I have placed Wall Letters on the gym walls, I attract the students' attention to them by using this game. For example, "Find the letter *s*," or "Find a purple letter," or "Find a letter that is in your first name." Or, with very young students, hold up a large Alphabet Letter Card and direct the children to "Find one that looks like this."

Directionality terms can be practiced with this game, too. Here is a sample of phrases that could be used to teach and reinforce spatial positioning and other concepts:

Find something that is below the basketball net (or below the letter *N*).
Find something that is above the bleachers.
Find a corner.
Find something that is between the clock and me.
Find something that is between the scoreboard and the soccer goal.
Find something that is vertical.

Find something that is horizontal.
Find something that is diagonal.
Find something square.
Find something with three sides.
Find something inside the basketball court.
Find something outside the basketball court.
Find something curvy.
Find something straight.
Find something near the exit door, volleyball net, or teacher's desk.
Find something that is over the door.
Find something that is next to the equipment closet.
Find something with a letter on it.
Find something with a number on it.
Find something that is far away from the equipment closet.
Find something that is very close to the desk.

Memory

Objectives: Letter Matching and Sound Naming
Equipment: Alphabet Letter Cards (two or more sets necessary)
Area: Classroom, Gymnasium, or Outdoors
Number of Participants: 1+
Grades: Pre-K–2

This game is commonly used as a board game, in which students sit and play at a table or on the floor. Our version of the game can involve walking and crawling over Alphabet Letter Cards and Word Cards, to find a match. Depending on the space available, a student can even run from one letter or word to another, searching for the match!

The object of the game is for a player to turn over two letters, as they are placed upside down, and then find a match. When a player finds a match, he keeps both cards and then his opponent takes her turn. Create a game in which the students involved are working on letters that they need to practice. Sometimes, a student will know the uppercase version of a letter but have difficulty identifying its lowercase counterpart. This game can be set up so that the match is the opposite case. In this example, individual packets of Alphabet Letter Cards are set up all over the play area, so that multiple games are occurring simultaneously.

Another variety of the game is to set up an Alphabet Sea in the room and have all players simply search for as many matches as possible. Again, rules can be made so that a player must find one uppercase and one lowercase version of the same letter to have a match. You could also furnish students with a list of letters that they are to find, rather than having them search aimlessly for only the letters for which they are already familiar.

Try ending Memory with some form of sharing. Sometimes the students must tell the leader or another helper all of the letters found and the sounds those letters make. Some students may even be able to tell words that begin with the letter or sound of the letters found!

Finally, encourage counting whenever possible and as time allows. For example, you can have students count the number of letters or pairs found, before turning them in. Also, ask students to collect the remaining letters on the floor not used in the game; these letters can be counted, too, before being placed in the box.

Simon Says

> **Objectives:** Letter Recognition, Body Parts Identification, and Directionality
> **Equipment:** None
> **Area:** Classroom, Hallway, Gymnasium, or Outdoors
> **Number of Participants:** 1+
> **Grades:** K–2

Simon Says needs no explanation, but this is a wonderful game to teach body parts, spatial concepts, directionality terms, and colors. For example, "Simon Says touch your left elbow to your right knee" or "Simon Says sit far away from the door." If you have displayed or arranged alphabet letters in the play area, they can also be used to reinforce alphabet letter identification or word identification. For example, "Simon Says find and touch the letter *r*" or "Simon Says create the word *cat* using the letters on the floor." To reinforce personal information, "Simon Says find the first letter of your middle name." If you change the task often enough, all students will be engaged and no students will need to be eliminated from the game. This is desired, as often the students who are eliminated are the very ones who need the most practice. Therefore, when playing Simon Says, keep in mind the objective: helping the students to learn, not ending the game with one winner.

Line Tag

> **Objectives:** Letter Matching and Sound Recognition
> **Equipment:** None, except a line for the chasers to play on (and possibly Alphabet Letter Cards)
> **Area:** Gymnasium or Outdoors
> **Number of Participants:** 5+
> **Grades:** K–2

In this tagging game, a line is used for the chasers to run along; at our school, we usually use the centerline on the basketball court. All other players stand at a predetermined area from the centerline, perhaps an end line. The chaser calls out a letter of the alphabet. Any players who have that letter in their first name must run to the other predetermined area opposite the centerline. At that point, the chaser attempts to tag all players running. Those who are tagged become chasers and join on the centerline. All chasers may run along the centerline, but they may not leave the centerline. Another letter is called, and again, any player who is not a chaser must run to the opposite side if that letter is in their first name. Players are now possibly running from both directions, as players must always run to the opposite side they are currently on if their letter is called.

If space allows, a middle area can be designated the "chaser zone," where instead of running along a line, the chasers must remain within a rectangular area but are free to run anywhere in that box.

The teacher may change the rules to include a letter that appears in your first and last names or in a player's first, middle, and last names. The teacher may use sounds rather than letters: the chaser makes the sound of a letter, and if a student has that sound in their name, she must run. Blends and diagraphs may also be used.

Another version for letter recognition is to have the chaser select an alphabet card from a box of letters and then show this card to the players. Any player who has this letter shown in his name must run. This would work best if there is more than one chaser, as a solo chaser may find it difficult to run, tag, and hold the letter, because players are sure to take off as soon as they recognize the letter.

Be sure to review safety measures when students are running from both directions; you don't want anyone to run into someone else!

Bean Bag Toss

> **Objectives:** Rhyming, Phonemic Blending, Sound Recognition,
> Word Spelling, and Word Creation
> **Equipment:** Bean Bags (or Yarn Balls, Trash Balls, etc.), Cardboard
> Box, Paper, and Markers
> **Area:** Classroom, Hallways, Gymnasium, or Outdoors
> **Number of Participants:** 1+
> **Grades:** K–2

You will need a large box (we use computer boxes) or some other large target that is developmentally appropriate to your students. Write a simple word large enough to cover most of the space on the side of the box. Tape the word to the side of the box facing the students. Omit the first letter of the word, so the word *hat* would appear as *-at*. The object of the game is for each student to take a turn tossing a bean bag or other item into the box. Each time a student reaches the goal of getting the bean bag into the box, that student has a chance to add a letter to the front of the word to create a new word. Essentially, the students are working with word onsets and rimes. For example, a student who tosses her bean bag into the box might select the consonant sound /m/ and blend it with the rime *-at* forming the word *mat*. Students can take turns writing their words on the list that their group is creating.

You can simply play this game for the fun of the tossing and creating new words, or you can add the competitive element. When competing, students may try to form more words than the other players at their boxes. Another form of competing is to have multiple bean bag toss stations set up in the play area; each group works together to try to form more words than other groups. Kids enjoy making real words that they use in their everyday language, as well as nonsense words. Count them all!

Alphabet Letter Scavenger Hunt

> **Objectives:** Alphabetic Sequencing, Letter Matching, Letter Recognition, Sound Recognition, and Sound Matching
> **Equipment:** Alphabet Letter Cards (two or more sets may be necessary)
> **Area:** Outdoors
> **Number of Participants:** 1+
> **Grades:** K–3

Scatter or hide Alphabet Letter Cards in an area outdoors. Have students work alone or in pairs to search for letters. You can scatter enough letters so that each student or pair must find all letters to make one complete alphabet set. You can give students or pairs a list of letters that they must find; this is an easy way to individualize instruction so that each student is working on the letters he or she is struggling with at the time of the game. If students are very young, you could have them find one letter at a time, bringing them to you and identifying them before going for more. You could give the sound of a letter and they must find the letter to match it. Depending on the items in the area where you play the game, students could also find and bring along something that begins with the sound of the letter found.

Word Scavenger Hunt

> **Objectives:** Letter Naming, Sound Naming, Word Copying, Word Creation, and Word Spelling
> **Equipment:** Alphabet Letter Cards (two or more sets necessary) and Word Cards
> **Area:** Outdoors
> **Number of Participants:** 1+
> **Grades:** K–3

This game is similar to Alphabet Letter Scavenger Hunt. Scatter or hide Alphabet Letter Cards around the play area. Students may work alone or in pairs to seek out letters and then try to form a word with the found letters. You can give each student or pair of students a word card and have them search for the Alphabet Letter Cards needed to create that word. Designate an area nearby where students or pairs come to lay out the letters in the correct order to make the word on the card. You can easily check off letters and words for assessment with this game, if each student works independently and has an area designated for his or her letters.

Some students will finish earlier than others; give these students another word to find. Sometimes you can let them select a word from a word pile, and other times you can select the word for them. These students may be able to find enough words that they can form sentences.

You might have some students in your class playing this game, while others will still be playing Alphabet Letter Scavenger Hunt. Both can be played simultaneously, allowing you to meet everyone's needs.

Barnyard Game

Objective: Sound Matching
Equipment: None
Area: Classroom, Gymnasium, or Outdoors
Number of Participants: 4+
Grades: K–3

The Barnyard Game is a traditional game played at many parties, often as an icebreaker to social activity. In the traditional game, a leader in the group whispers the name of an animal into the ear of each member playing the game. Cow, dog, cat, and pig are commonly used. When everyone has been given a secret animal, the leader instructs each player to make the noise of the given animal, with the objective being to find like animals. Ideally, the game ends when each player is within the group of his or her animal; cows are together in a group, cats are together in a group, and so forth.

This version of the game is quite similar, except that players are given a letter of the alphabet to use rather than an animal name, to find like members. When the teacher has given a variety of letters by whispering into players' ears, the players make the sound of that letter in order to find their group.

The teacher may play this game in a variety of ways. For instance, letters may be randomly chosen or letters may be all vowels whispered into players' ears. Letters may be those letters being taught at the present, including ones already learned for review. Letters may be those that students are struggling with and require greater reinforcement.

The teacher may also expand this game to include blends and diagraphs, such as the H Brothers, rather than individual alphabet letters. Puzzles is a great follow-up activity to this game, if students are capable of word formation.

Letter Twister

Objectives: Letter Matching and Word Matching
Equipment: Letter Twister Mat, Alphabet Letter Cards, and Word
 Cards
Area: Classroom, Hallway, Gymnasium, or Outdoors
Number of Participants: 1+
Grades: K–3

Letter Twister is a spin-off of the home entertainment game, only adapted
for use with letters and words. Take an old Twister game mat and add a
letter to each circle, to make a Letter Twister mat. Have students play by
selecting an Alphabet Letter Card from a pile, then search for that letter
on the mat, and place a body part on it. Another student may take a turn,
you may join them, or they may continue playing the game alone. Be
sure that the letters on the mat match the letters in the Alphabet Letter
Card pile. You can tape letters onto the mat, so that the tape can be re-
moved and changed as the students learn more letters or require practice
with certain ones.

  If you do not have a Twister mat, one can easily be made by using a
disposable tablecloth. The flannel-backed tablecloths fold well and last
a long time. Making a Twister mat of your own also allows the circles
to be placed closer together if necessary for the small size of players.
For an entire class of students to play, many Twister mats can be placed
about the room, with students playing one game, then moving along to
play again at another mat, where the letters are different.

  This game can also be played using a word, rather than a letter, in
each circle. The student selects a Word Card from the pile of words,
places a body part on the circle, and the game continues. Again, be certain that the Word Cards match the words on the mat.

Alphabet Tag

Objectives: Letter Forming, Letter Naming, and Sound Recognition
Equipment: None
Area: Gymnasium or Outdoors
Number of Participants: 5+
Grades: K–5

Alphabet Tag is a basic chase game, with one or more students designated the chaser or "it." The number of chasers is dependent on the number of players and the players' age and ability level. The game is similar to Freeze Tag, except in this version, the player tagged "freezes" in the shape of a letter of the alphabet (of his or her choice). That player remains frozen until another player in the game guesses what letter he or she has formed. If the guessing player cannot guess in three tries, the frozen player may give a hint by telling the sound this letter makes. Of course, other players may come over and help out, too.

Sometimes, the students may need some help in selecting a letter to freeze as, when tagged. You might suggest that they freeze, when tagged, as letters in their first or last names or as the letters posted. On the chalkboard, post all the letters learned so far or those posing difficulties.

Writing Relays

>   **Objectives:** Letter Naming, Sound Naming, Word Spelling, and
>   Word Creation
>   **Equipment:** Hula Hoops, Alphabet Letter Cards, Scooter Boards,
>   Jump Ropes, Word Cards, and boxes
>   **Area:** Gymnasium or Outdoors
>   **Number of Participants:** 2+
>   **Grades:** 1–5

This game is adapted from a holiday activity called Reindeer Relays, sometimes played prior to winter vacation. Students are in relay formation, approximately four students per team. Each team has an empty box, scooter board, and jump rope. One student sits on the scooter board holding one end of the jump rope. A second student stands out in front of the scooter board, holding the other end of the jump rope. On the "Go" signal, the "Rudolph" student pulls the "sleigh" with "Santa" to the North Pole. The North Pole is located at the other side of the gym, across from the group. Each team has its own "North Pole." The North Pole is a hula hoop filled with twenty or more pieces of physical education equipment taken from the storage closet. The task at the North Pole is for the pair of students to select one "toy" to take back to the group; the two also switch Rudolph and Santa roles. Upon returning to the group, the pair "drops the toy down the chimney" by placing it into the box. The next pair takes its turn and the game continues until all toys have been gotten from the North Pole.

In the adapted version of this game, the hula hoop is filled with three or more sets of alphabet letters. Pairs of students have their own "North Pole" and their task is to form a word. Typically, you would give a Word Card to the pair and ask that each student take turns going to the hoop, riding and pulling, collecting all necessary letters to create the word given on the card. Once all the necessary letters are obtained, the students either work together or take turns to place the letters in the correct order. Once you have checked that the letters are in their proper order, ask the name of each letter, the sound it makes, and what word they have spelled. Once this word has been completed, give a new word. Some pairs of students will require more challenging words than other pairs.

Life-Size Bingo

Objectives: Letter Recognition, Sound Recognition, and Word Matching
Equipment: Tablecloths, Alphabet Letter Cards, and Bean Bags
Area: Classroom, Hallway, Gymnasium, or Outdoors
Number of Participants: 2+
Grades: 1–5

Life-Size Bingo uses alphabet letters, rather than numbers, in the squares on the card. Make the life-size cards by using inexpensive picnic tablecloths. The flannel-backed ones are a little more expensive than the plastic ones, but they will last a lot longer in the long run. You can draw the Life-Size Bingo grid on the tablecloth or use an opaque projector for tracing from a real bingo card. Students may use bean bags to mark the squares on the bingo card that have been called.

Students may play individually or in pairs. The teacher or another student may select letters randomly from a pile or box or bucket of letters. The letter selected is called out to the players. All players who have the selected letter anywhere on their playing card may mark it by tossing a bean bag into that square. A player or pair of players wins if they attain a row, column, or other designation, as in traditional Bingo.

A variety of Life-Size Bingo cards can be made for different purposes. Some reinforce all alphabet letters, some only vowels or consonants. Some Life-Size Bingo cards might be made to reinforce letters that have been taught in the classroom to a given point. You can adapt Bingo cards using Velcro to individualize instruction. For example, a Life-Size Bingo card that has been created with a variety of letters on it can be adapted to focus on only those letters posing difficulty for students. Attach the letters with a piece of Velcro (or tape if using the plastic tablecloths). Be sure that the pile or bucket or box of letters from which the randomly selected letters are called is tailored to the Life-Size Bingo cards.

Letters for Sale

Objectives: Sound Matching and Sound Recognition
Equipment: None
Area: Gymnasium or Outdoors
Number of Participants: 4+
Grades: 1–5

This is a tag game that requires four bases in each corner of the play space. The chaser, or "it," is in the center of the play space. Players are divided and placed into three of the four bases. Each group is given the name of an alphabet letter. The chaser calls out one of the given letters, and then all of the students in that group flee to the open or empty base. The chaser attempts to chase and tag these runners. Any tagged player joins the chaser in the center for the remainder of the game. Next, the chaser calls out another one of the alphabet letters and chases the players designated as that letter. Again, all tagged players join the chaser in the center. The game continues until all players are tagged or only one player of a given letter remains.

Although we have mentioned corners for the location of the bases, be sure to move the base far enough away from the corner to avoid students' running into the wall. We usually tape a large square on the floor or place a large hula hoop if playing with only a small group of students for the base, so students have plenty of room to be "safe."

Once the students understand how the game is played, try varying the rules. The chaser may call out the sound of a letter, rather than naming the letter, to identify which group must run to a new base. Also, the chase can call out a word that begins with the letter of the group to be chases. Sometimes you may need to give the chaser the word to use, at least initially, and sometimes the chaser may catch on right away and come up with words on her own. Groups can be assigned blends and diagraphs like the H Brothers[4] instead of individual letters. You can make things really tricky by having a /ph/ group and an /f/ group and using words like *fire* and *phone*.

Mickey Mouse and Minnie, Too

Objectives: Letter Naming, Sound Naming, and Word Creation
Equipment: 4 Hula Hoops, Alphabet Letter Cards, and Word Cards
Area: Gymnasium or Outdoors
Number of Participants: 4+
Grades: 1–5

A retired colleague left many books and records that she had collected over her years as a physical education teacher. "Mickey Mouse"[5] appeared in an old textbook, and we play it with students in grades 1 and 2. With a little creativity, the game can be used to work with struggling readers who like to run and move and shout.

Mickey Mouse and Minnie, Too is played using a square or rectangle. The basketball court boundaries work well for this game. Divide the group into four teams, and place one team on each line of the rectangle. Place four hula hoops in the center of the square, each containing one or two sets of Alphabet Letter Cards. Each team uses a hula hoop of its own, which team members run to when it is their turn. Give each child on each team a number, so that there are four 1s, four 2s, four 3s, and so forth.

Begin the game by calling the number 1. All the students designated as the number 1 leave their places and run around the outside of the square. Next, they run to their team's hula hoop, entering the inside of the rectangle through the opening where they had been standing. Upon reaching the hoop, the student takes a letter, returns to the teammates, and tell them what letter it is and what sound it makes. Next, the student comes to you to report the same information. At this point, you can take the letter, or it can be returned to the hoop or placed in a designated area with the team. Repeat the activity by calling another number.

The game ends when all students have had numerous turns to run and select a letter. The game can take a new twist if you have asked the teams to keep the obtained letters in some designated place. At this point, have the team gather together to create any and all words possible with the pile of letters.

Another variation to this game is to place Word Cards in the hula hoop instead of Alphabet Letter Cards. The students select a word, return to their teams, and tell the word, how to spell it, and use it in a sentence. Again, the words can be returned to the hula hoops, to the teacher, or to a designated place near the team. If kept, the words can be used to form sentences at the end of the running portion of the game. If this option is used, be sure that a variety of words are put in the hula hoop so that students have the possibility of making a simple but coherent sentence.

Finally, play the game enough times that all of the students understand the gist, and then change how you call out the number. Instead of saying "Three's," try "One plus two" or "Number of adults in the room right now" or some other thinking statement. This helps to keep all of the students paying attention and thinking as well as helping one another to solve the problem of who gets to take his or her turn.

Writing Red Rover

Objectives: Word Copying and Word Creation
Equipment: Buckets or Boxes, Alphabet Letter Cards, Paper, and
   Pencils or Chalk
Area: Classroom, Gymnasium, or Outdoors
Number of Participants: 4+
Grades: 1–5

This traditional game from the playgrounds of yesteryear has been altered to make it not only safe but also educational. The tradition of
holding on tightly to keep the player from "breaking through" has been
eliminated from the game. In this version, the team chanting a name
wants the player to make it over!

Create two teams consisting of about two or three players. Each
team is given a bucket filled with Alphabet Letter Cards that you have
hand-selected. Choose different letters for each bucket, but attempt to
keep the level of difficulty similar for each team. Place the teams with
their buckets about twenty feet apart. Give the teams about five minutes to create as many words as possible from the given letters. Next,
the team that has created the least number of words gets to ask for help
from the other team by calling, "Red Rover, Red Rover, let Katie come
over." "Katie" gets to join the other team to offer help. After a few
minutes of work, the other team gets to ask for help with the same
chant. Only allow a team to ask for a person for a second time after
everyone has already been called and given the chance to help out the
other team. The purpose for allowing the players to switch teams is to
let someone who has not been staring at the same letters to provide
some fresh insight, while using the chant from an old game rarely seen
anymore.

It may be helpful to allow one of the team members to record each
word that is found to eliminate repetition of words; especially since
team members will be alternating. This recorder can be someone who
is a natural leader, someone who needs help with writing skills, someone who may be able to provide the most help to the team via record-
ing rather than creating words, or the job may rotate from player to
player as the words are discovered. You may also give teams pencils

and scrap paper and allow them to write with chalk directly on the floor. As space permits, the words can be written using jump ropes.

Finally, the students love when we add a river to jump when they cross over to the other side. Borrowing from the game Jump the River used when working on jumping skills in physical education class, create a river using two long ropes. The river varies in width, allowing for jumpers of all abilities to be challenged as their own level. This addition adds to the movement and excitement of the game!

Alphabet Soup

> **Objectives:** Letter Naming, Sound Matching, and Sound Recognition
> **Equipment:** Chair (or something for each student to sit on) and Alphabet Letter Cards
> **Area:** Classroom, Gymnasium, or Outdoors
> **Number of Participants:** 6+
> **Grades:** 1–5

Alphabet Soup is an adaptation of the game called Fruit Salad, which can be found in *Games We Should Play in School,* by Frank Aycox.[6]

In Alphabet Soup, all players except one need a chair of their own. When playing in the gym, give each player a hula hoop to sit in rather than a chair. You could also use carpet squares or poly-spots instead of chairs. All of the chairs, or hula-hoops, are placed in a circle.

Next, ask the players to think of the name of an alphabet letter, which they are to remember for the entire game. Tell the students that the name of the alphabet letter that they have selected is a secret; like any secret, you remember it and do not tell anyone else. One player, probably you when teaching the game for the first time, starts in the center of the circle without a chair or hula hoop. The object of the game for this person is try to get a chair or hula hoop. To do so, this person in the center calls out the name of one, two, or three alphabet letters. The rule is that any player who has the letters called, as their secret, must get up and find a new chair or hula hoop to sit on. These players who must move only need to find a different seat than the one they previously occupied but not announce their letters, it is a secret until the end of the game. At this point, this is the opportunity for the player in the center to move to one of the available seats before someone else does.

The player in the center may also use the option of calling, "Alphabet soup." When "Alphabet soup" is called, *all* players must get up and find a new seat. Continue playing as long as everyone is engaged in the activity. At the conclusion of the game, have everyone go around the circle and reveal the name of his or her alphabet letter.

An alternative way to play is to have the player in the center say the sound of the letters, rather than the name of the letter. If the group is small in number, you might limit the letters to vowels or letters you have practiced so far. Players could also show an Alphabet Letter Card, rather than say the names of letters, when in the center of the circle.

Four Square Sound-Off

Objective: Alphabetic Sequencing
Equipment: Playground Ball and Four Square Grid
Area: Gymnasium or Outdoors
Number of Participants: 4+
Grades: 2–5

This is the traditional Four Square game with an alphabet component added. The server begins the game and says the letter *A*. The next player to receive the ball must play the ball as is normally played in traditional Four Square and also say the letter *B*. The next player to receive the ball must play the ball as is normally played in traditional Four Square and also say the letter *C*. The game ends when a player makes an error with the ball or fails to state the next letter of the alphabet, in the correct order. Attempt to play a round so that all players, together, can get to *Z*.

A variation of this game is to have the server pick any letter of the alphabet to begin the game. If the server begins the game with the letter *M*, then the next player to receive the ball must say *N*. All players continue along the alphabet from where the server begins. If the players continue to *Z*, they wrap around to *A*. A victory is achieved when the players are able to go through the entire alphabet and back to the server's starting letter.

Four Square Word Builder

> **Objectives:** Word Creation and Word Spelling
> **Equipment:** Playground Ball and Four Square Grid
> **Area:** Gymnasium or Outdoors
> **Number of Participants:** 4+
> **Grades:** 2–5

Play the traditional Four Square game. Add the rule to the game that when the server begins the game, he or she must say a letter of the alphabet. The next player to receive the ball must play the ball as is normally played in traditional Four Square and also say another letter of the alphabet, in attempt to begin to form a word. The next player to receive the ball must play the ball as is normally played in traditional Four Square and also say another letter of the alphabet, in efforts to complete or continue the formation of a word. For example, if the server begins the game and says the letter *R,* the player to receive the serve might say the letter *E.* The next player to receive the ball could say the letter *D* to complete the word *red.* At this point, the players have won by forming a word. If a player makes an error with the ball or by stating a letter that would not help in the formation of a word, that player is out and moves to the end of the line.

This game can also be used as a way to practice spelling words. In this variation, the teacher gives the server a spelling word, and the game proceeds as above with each player providing the next letter in the word.

NOTES

1. Nancy E. Hungerford, Sandra L. Peters, and Carol J. Myers, *Movement Activities for the Young Child* (Lancaster, Pa.: The Copy Shop, Student Services: Millersville University, 1992), 117.

2. Victoria E. Greene and Mary Lee Enfield, *Phonology Guide, Project Read* (Bloomington, Minn.: Language Circle Enterprises, 1991), 15–2.

3. Marianne Torbert and Lynne B. Schneider, *Follow Me, Too* (Philadelphia: Leonard Gordon Institute of Human Development, draft version for Addison-Wesley, January 1992), 65.

4. Greene and Enfield, *Phonology Guide, Project Read,* 11:1.

5. Victor P. Dauer, *Dynamic Physical Education for Elementary School Children,* 4th ed. (Minneapolis: Burgess, 1971), 306.

6. Frank Aycox, *Games We Should Play in School* (Byron, Calif.: First Row Experience, 1985), 32.

Activities and Games by Grade Level

Grade Level Page	Activity/Game	Skill	
Pre-K–2	*Alphabet Sea	AS, LC, LM, LR, LN, SM, SR, SN, WC, WCr, WS, WM	40
	Identify a Letter	LM, LR, LN, SR, SN	43
	*Memory	LM, SN	69
	Create a Letter	LC, LN, SR	45
Pre-K–3	Jumping Jellybeans . . . and Elephants, Too!	SySeg, SeSeg, Pseg	46
Pre-K–5	Find It	LM, LR, SR, Dir	67
K–2	Create an Alphabet	AS, LC, LR, SN	49
	Line Tag	LM, SR	71
	ABC Order	AS, LM, LR, LN, SM, SN	48
	*Jump Rope Roundup	LC, LM, LN, SM, SN	52
	*52 Pickup	AS, LM, LR, LN, SN, WS	50
	*Twist and Shout	LC, LN, SM, SR, SN, WC, WS	56
	Sandman	LC, LN, SM, SR, SN, WC, WS, WCr	51
	*Fun with Chalk	LC, LR, LN, SR, SM, WC, WS	53
	Fun with Paintbrushes	LC, LN, SR, SM, WC, WS	55
	Speed Racer	LC, SR, WS, Dir	54
	Simon Says	LR, BP, Dir	70
	Bean Bag Toss	R, PB, SR, WS	72
K–3	Barnyard Game	SM	75
	*Alphabet Letter Scavenger Hunt	AS, LM, LR, SR, SM	73
	*Word Scavenger Hunt	LN, SN, WCr, WC, WS	74
	Letter Twister	LM, WM	76
K–5	*Read and Run	AS, LR, LN, SN	57
	Connect the Dots	AS, LR, LN, SN	59
	Alphabet Tag	LF, LN, SR	77
	Tracing with Chalk	LC, LN, LR, SM, SR	58

Grade Level Page	Activity/Game	Skill	
	*Wash Line	LM, LR, LN, SR, WC, WS	60
	Body Cutouts	LC, LN, WS	61
	Puzzles	LR, SN, PB, WCr	63
	Mystery Writer	LC, LN, SR, WC	62
1–5	Writing Relays	LN, SN, WS, WCr	78
	Group Word Formation	WC, WS	64
	Word Scramble	WCr, WS, LC, R	65
	Life-Size Bingo	LR, SR, WM	79
	Letters for Sale	SM, SR	80
	Alphabet Soup	LN, SM, SR	85
	Mickey Mouse and Minnie, Too!	LN, SN, WCr	81
	Writing Red Rover	WC, WCr	83
2–5	Four Square Sound-Off	AS	87
	Four Square Word Builder	WS, WCr	88

Key: AS = Alphabetic Sequencing, BP = Body Parts Identification, Dir = Directionality, LC = Letter Copying, LF = Letter Forming, LM = Letter Matching, LN = Letter Naming, LR = Letter Recognition, PB = Phonemic Blending, Pseg = Phonemic Segmentation, R = Rhyming, SM = Sound Matching, SR = Sound Recognition, SN = Sound Naming, SeSeg = Sentence Segmentation, SySeg = Syllable Segmentation, WC = Word Copying, WCr = Word Creation, WM = Word Matching, and WS = Word Spelling.
*Denotes a game or activity that can be used as an assessment tool.

Activities and Games by Skill

Skill	Activity/Game	Grade	Page
Alphabetic Sequencing	Alphabet Sea	Pre-K–2	40
	ABC Order	K–2	48
	Create an Alphabet	K–2	49
	52 Pickup	K–2	50
	Alphabet Letter Scavenger Hunt	K–3	73
	Read and Run	K–5	57
	Connect the Dots	K–5	59
	Four Square Sound-Off	2–5	87
Letter Copying	Alphabet Sea	Pre-K–2	40
	Create a Letter	Pre-K–2	45
	Jump Rope Roundup	K–2	52
	Speed Racer	K–2	54
	Fun with Chalk	K–2	53
	Fun with Paintbrushes	K–2	55
	Create an Alphabet	K–2	49
	Sandman	K–2	51
	Twist and Shout	K–2	56
	Body Cutouts	K–5	61
	Mystery Writer	K–5	62
	Tracing with Chalk	K–5	58
	Word Scramble	1–5	65
Letter Matching	Alphabet Sea	Pre-K–2	40
	Identify a Letter	Pre-K–2	43
	Memory	Pre-K–2	69
	Find It	Pre-K–5	67
	ABC Order	K–2	48
	52 Pickup	K–2	50
	Line Tag	K–2	71
	Jump Rope Roundup	K–2	52
	Letter Twister	K–3	76
	Alphabet Letter Scavenger Hunt	K–3	73
	Wash Line	K–5	60

Skill	Activity/Game	Grade	Page
Letter Recognition	Alphabet Sea	Pre-K–2	40
	Identify a Letter	Pre-K–2	43
	Find It	Pre-K–5	67
	ABC Order	K–2	48
	52 Pickup	K–2	50
	Create an Alphabet	K–2	49
	Simon Says	K–2	70
	Fun with Chalk	K–2	53
	Alphabet Letter Scavenger Hunt	K–3	73
	Read and Run	K–5	57
	Tracing with Chalk	K–5	58
	Wash Line	K–5	60
	Connect the Dots	K–5	59
	Puzzles	K–5	63
	Life-Size Bingo	1–5	79
Letter Forming	Alphabet Tag	K–5	77
Letter Naming	Alphabet Sea	Pre-K–2	40
	Create a Letter	Pre-K–2	45
	Identify a Letter	Pre-K–2	43
	ABC Order	K–2	48
	52 Pickup	K–2	50
	Sandman	K–2	51
	Fun with Chalk	K–2	53
	Fun with Paintbrushes	K–2	55
	Jump Rope Roundup	K–2	52
	Twist and Shout	K–2	56
	Word Scavenger Hunt	K–3	74
	Tracing with Chalk	K–5	58
	Read and Run	K–5	57
	Connect the Dots	K–5	59
	Mystery Writer	K–5	62
	Body Cutouts	K–5	61
	Wash Line	K–5	60
	Alphabet Tag	K–5	77
	Writing Relays	1–5	78
	Mickey Mouse and Minnie, Too	1–5	81
	Alphabet Soup	1–5	85
Sound Recognition	Alphabet Sea	Pre-K–2	40
	Create a Letter	Pre-K–2	45
	Identify a Letter	Pre-K–2	43
	Find It	Pre-K–5	67
	Sandman	K–2	51
	Speed Racer	K–2	54
	Fun with Chalk	K–2	53
	Fun with Paintbrushes	K–2	55
	Line Tag	K–2	71
	Twist and Shout	K–2	56

Skill	Activity/Game	Grade	Page
	Fun with Chalk	K–2	53
	Twist and Shout	K–2	56
	Sandman	K–2	51
	Fun with Paintbrushes	K–2	55
	Word Scavenger Hunt	K–3	74
	Mystery Writer	K–5	62
	Wash Line	K–5	60
	Writing Red Rover	1–5	83
	Group Word Formation	1–5	64
Word Spelling	Alphabet Sea	Pre-K–2	40
	Sandman	K–2	51
	Speed Racer	K–2	54
	Fun with Chalk	K–2	53
	Twist and Shout	K–2	56
	Fun with Paintbrushes	K–2	55
	52 Pickup	K–2	50
	Bean Bag Toss	K–2	72
	Word Scavenger Hunt	K–3	74
	Wash Line	K–5	60
	Body Cutouts	K–5	61
	Writing Relays	1–5	78
	Group Word Formation	1–5	64
	Word Scramble	1–5	65
	Four Square Word Builder	2–5	87
Word Matching	Alphabet Sea	Pre-K–2	40
	Letter Twister	K–3	76
	Life-Size Bingo	1–5	79
Word Creation	Alphabet Sea	Pre-K–2	40
	Sandman	K–2	51
	Word Scavenger Hunt	K–3	74
	Puzzles	K–5	63
	Writing Relays	1–5	78
	Word Scramble	1–5	65
	Writing Red Rover	1–5	83
	Mickey Mouse and Minnie, Too	1–5	81
	Four Square Word Builder	2–5	87
Sentence Segmentation	Jumping Jellybeans . . . and Elephants, Too!	Pre-K–3	46
Directionality Terms	Find It	Pre-K–2	67
	Simon Says	K–2	70
	Speed Racer	K–2	54
Body Parts Identification	Simon Says	K–2	70

Making Alphabet Letter and Word Cards

As you can see, now that you have perused the games and activities in this book, Alphabet Letter Cards and Word Cards are necessary materials. The cards we have used are homemade. We are fortunate to have what is known as an Ellison Machine in our school. The machine is a die cutter, and we have alphabet letter dies available in various sizes. We use the four-inch high letters. The letters are cut out of construction paper and then mounted on a square of construction paper in a contrasting color. Because our cards are used frequently by lots of little hands, we have chosen to laminate them. We also have a set of large Alphabet Letter Cards that we use as stimulus cards — cards we hold up to cue the students. These are ten-inch high block letters glued onto a standard size piece of construction paper. These cards are also laminated to make them last longer.

Most teachers will have available to them everything they need to make their own letter cards. If an Ellison Machine is not available, stencils most likely are. Parents will have to go to more trouble and expense to make their alphabet cards. We have found an on-line source[1] that sells precut, four-inch high letters in a variety of colors and materials that could easily be mounted on construction paper or oak tag. The cards take time to make, but it is well worth it because once made and laminated, they last for quite a while. The more sets of letter cards you have available, the more you will be able to do.

The Word Cards are simply rectangular pieces of construction paper or oak tag on which we write words with magic markers. The words on the cards may be sight words (words that do no follow decoding rules or that are used so frequently that it is necessary to know them automatically by sight), spelling words, or other words designated by the classroom teacher. Words that we typically use include Dolch Words, color and number words, directionality and spatial terms, and movement words (see appendix D for lists). If you are a parent or physical education teacher, you will want to be sure to consult with the children's classroom teachers to be sure you are practicing the correct words.

NOTE

1. Precut letters can be purchased from The Learning Source at www.edumart. com.

Word Lists

DOLCH WORDS

Dolch words[1] are those words children will most frequently encounter when learning to read. The words are arranged in order of frequency. There are 220 Dolch words in all, and many do not follow normal decoding patterns. Whether they are decodable or not, these are words that should become automatic for children if they are to become fluent beginning readers. The eleven lists of Dolch Words presented here are a good starting place for making Word Cards.

List 1

the	to	and	he	a	I	you	it	of	in
was	said	his	that	she	for	on	they	but	had

List 2

at	him	with	up	all	look	is	her	there	some
out	as	be	have	go	we	am	then	little	down

List 3

do	can	could	when	did	what	so	see	not	were
get	them	like	one	this	my	would	me	will	yes

List 4

| big | went | are | come | if | now | long | no | came | ask |
| very | an | over | your | its | ride | into | just | blue | red |

List 5

| from | good | any | about | around | want | don't | how | know | right |
| put | too | got | take | where | every | pretty | jump | green | four |

List 6

| away | old | by | their | here | saw | call | after | well | think |
| ran | let | help | make | going | sleep | brown | yellow | five | six |

List 7

| walk | two | or | before | eat | again | play | who | been | may |
| stop | off | never | seven | eight | cold | today | fly | myself | round |

List 8

| tell | much | keep | give | work | first | try | new | must | start |
| black | white | ten | does | bring | goes | write | always | drink | once |

List 9

| soon | made | run | gave | open | has | find | only | us | three |
| our | better | hold | buy | funny | warm | ate | full | those | done |

List 10

| use | fast | say | light | pick | hurt | pull | cut | kind | both |
| sit | which | fall | carry | small | under | read | why | own | found |

List 11

wash	show	hot	far	live	draw	clean	grow	best	because
upon	these	sing	please	thank	wish	many	shall	laugh	together

Spatial Words

above	below	under	over	beneath
next to	far	near	between	close
away	toward	behind	there	here
left	right	back	front	diagonal
horizontal	vertical	high	low	

Movement Words

run	walk	gallop	skip	hop
fast	slow	jump	leap	sit
stand	kneel	crawl	slither	climb

NOTE

1. These lists of Dolch Words were found on the Internet at www. theschoolbell.com.

Bibliography

Adams, Marilyn Jager. *Beginning to Read*. Cambridge, Mass.: MIT Press, 1999.

Armstrong, Thomas. *Multiple Intelligences in the Classroom*. Alexandria, Va.: Association for Supervision and Curriculum Development, 1994.

Aycox, Frank. *Games We Should Play in School*. Byron, Calif.: First Row Experience, 1985.

Black, Susan. "The First Two R's." *American School Board Journal* 186, no. 10 (1999): 44–46.

Braio, A., et al. "Incremental Implementation of Learning Style Strategies among Urban Low Achievers." *Journal of Educational Research* 91, no. 3 (1997).

Caine, Renate Nummela, and Geoffrey Caine. "Brain Based Learning: How the Brain Works," 1994, http://www.cainelearning.com [accessed on 10 Feb. 2001].

Cheney, Wendy, and Judith Cohen. *Focus on Phonics: Assessment and Instruction*. Bothell, Wash.: Wright/McGraw-Hill, 1999.

Dauer, Victor. *Dynamic Physical Education for Elementary Children,* 4th ed. Minneapolis: Burgess, 1971.

Delacato, Charles. *The Diagnosis and Treatment of Speech and Reading Problems*. Springfield, Ill.: Thomas, 1963.

Dennison, Paul, and Gail Dennison. *Brain Gym: Teacher's Edition, Revised*. Ventura, Calif.: Edu-Kinesthetics, 1990.

Dunn, Rita, and Kenneth Dunn. *Teaching Elementary Students through Their Individual Learning Styles: Practical Approaches for Grades 3–6*. Boston: Allyn & Bacon, 1993.

Dunn, Rita, Kenneth Dunn, and G. E. Price. *Learning Styles Inventory*. Lawrence, Kans.: Price Systems, 1989.

Flavell, John. *Cognitive Development,* 2d ed. Englewood Cliffs, N.J.: Prentice Hall, 1985.

Gardner, Howard. *The Disciplined Mind*. New York: Basic Books, 1999.

Greene, Victoria, and Mary Lee Enfield. *Phonology Guide, Project Read*. Bloomington, Minn.: Language Circle Enterprises, 1991.

Hungerford, Nancy E., Sandra L. Peters, and Carol J. Myers. *Movement Activities for the Young Child*. Lancaster, Pa: The Copy Shop, Student Services: Millersville University, 1992.

Jensen, Eric. "Moving with the Brain." *Educational Leadership* 58, no. 3 (2000): 34–37.

Kieff, Judith, and Renée Casbergue. *Playful Learning and Teaching: Integrating Play into Preschool and Primary Programs*. Boston: Allyn & Bacon, 2000.

Pellegrini, Anthony. *The Future of Play Theory*. Albany: State University of New York Press, 1995.

Reading Excellence Act. http://www.ed.gov/offices/OESE/REA/overview.html 1999 [accessed 10 Feb. 2001].

Snow, Rebecca. "Learning Styles in Young Children." http://earlychildhood .miningco.com/ 1999 [accessed 10 Feb. 2001].

Stone, Peter. "How We Turned Around a Problem School." *Principal* 72, no. 2 (1992): 34–36.

Torbert, Marianne, and Lynne Schneider. *Follow Me, Too*. Philadelphia: Gordon Leonard Institute for Play, January draft for Addison-Wesley, 1992.

Index

About the Authors

Tabatha A. Uhrich has taught physical education for eleven years at Union Canal Elementary School in Lebanon, Pennsylvania. She received her undergraduate degree in health and physical education at Virginia Commonwealth University and holds a master's degree from Penn State University. Currently, she is a doctoral student at Temple University in Philadelphia. Uhrich has coached field hockey at Cedar Crest High School and Lebanon Valley College. She has bicycled across the United States, plays golf, and enjoys mountain biking and skiing.

Monica McHale-Small has spent the last eleven years working as a school psychologist in Pennsylvania. Most of her experience has been at the elementary level, though she has had the opportunity to work with children from preschool age through high school. McHale-Small is also a part-time faculty member at Immaculata College where she teaches graduate courses in psychology and education. She received her master's degree and doctorate from the University of Pennsylvania, Graduate School of Education. When not involved in her professional pursuits, McHale-Small and her husband are kept busy parenting their four children, ages five through sixteen.